ADVANCED BEADWORK

by Ruth F. Poris

ACKNOWLEDGEMENTS

In the course of preparing this book, many people have graciously given their help and support. Rien Broer supplied the motivation; Wendy Owens and Patricia Woodbury generously lent their collections; Louis E. King gave both patience and skill; Chris Clor took elegant photos; Michael Poris and Laura Butler contributed their remarkable drawing talent; and husband, Bob, not only made the coffee, but prepared the entire manuscript for typesetting. My enduring thanks go to them, my parents, children and Elly and Lil.

Text and Illustrations ©1989 by Ruth F. Poris
All Rights Reserved.
3rd Printing 1991
ISBN 0-9616422-0-3
Library of Congress Catalog Card Number 90-81730
Printed in the United States of America.

All artwork by the author unless otherwise credited.
All photographs by Chris Clor.
Designed by Louis E. King

Published by:
Golden Hands Press
4202 Wateroak Lane
Tampa, FL 33624
(813) 265-1681

INTRODUCTION

This book grew slowly, from questions planted by readers of my previous book. It didn't seem to take long before short demonstrations became two day seminars, and then mimeographed instruction sheets. Finally, in self defense, a structured outline emerged.

My aim has been to organize all major beading techniques into one volume. In addition, I have tried to inspire experimentation, and to examine and end the "mystery" of drilling, sawing and soldering. I made no attempt to present numbered or graphed projects, since I deeply believe that all artists should explore and practice their craft until skills give wing to expression. Nor is this book meant to be a complete encyclopedia, as it is neither possible nor practical to cover every known procedure.

Based on my own personal methods and experience, each chapter is entirely devoted to similar skills. The drawings and photographs have been carefully designed to present each technique as clearly as possible.

It is my sincere hope that this book will inspire many hours of creative discovery, and bring you further along the road to an art born thousands of years ago.

Ruth J. Poris

January   1990

*"Every genuine work of art has as much reason for being
   as the earth and the sun"*

—Emerson

CONTENTS

CHAPTER 1

Materials & Tools

CHAPTER II

Threading Past The Basics

CHAPTER III

Off Loom Weaving

CHAPTER I
Materials & Tools

*Bone, Horn
& Bamboo on
Leather Cord
(Courtesy of
Wendy Owen)*

MATERIALS
BEADS

Let's start with the most basic necessity: BEADS! Available in all shapes, sizes, materials, colors,textures and styles, anything that suits your design, fits the technique being used and that strikes your fancy, is "right". A unique collection can be gathered from suppliers,from antique shows, garage sales, flea markets and old broken pieces from your grandma's attic. Those techniques which require specific kinds of beads will be described at the beginning of each chapter.

FINDINGS

The metal components that make jewelry wearable are called findings. Generally mass produced, they include anything that connects, fastens, extends, screws, pins or complements your necklace, bracelet, ring, earring, pin or pendent. Jewelry suppliers and craft shops usually stock a great variety of styles, metals and sizes. For those who desire to make their own handmade findings, chapters VII and VIII include clear instructions.

TOOLS

Very few tools are required for techniques included in this book, and since each chapter lists them, your own use will determine what you may have to buy. Before investing any money, look around your house and workspace, as you may already own some equipment. Tools can be added as needed, and many are interchangeable. Since their price is nominal, buying the best quality is always a wise choice.

CHAPTER II

Threading Past
The Basics

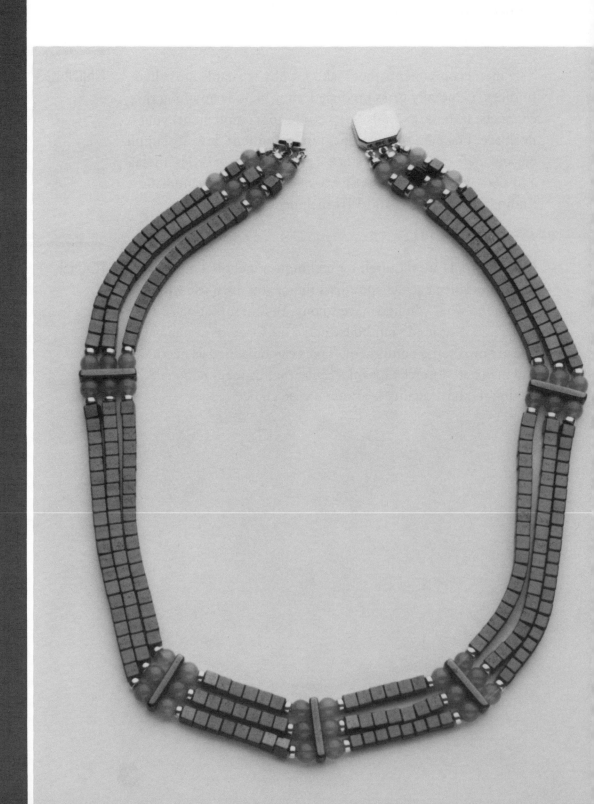

Choker, Hematite,
Grey Agate, Sterling

Years ago, after three working days spent knotting my first pearl necklace, I decided that beadstringing didn't require patience, but rather that it inspired patience and contributed to a healthy discipline of the hands, eyes and mind. A string of beads can be just that - a single thread on which beads are strung, or a complex design incorporating beautiful materials and finely honed skills.

How many times have you attempted a conceptual design, only to be stopped by lack of skills? Those are the times that try our patience! The following procedures are meant to soothe the spirit and add new dimension to your work. Utilize them for bracelets or necklaces.

EQUIPMENT AND SUPPLIES

Assuming that you've been stringing for awhile, most of the tools and supplies used in this chapter will already be in your workroom. Scissors, measuring implements, assorted needles and threads, crystal cement and glue are items used from project to project.

The techniques which follow may require some additional supplies: Multistrand clasps, Bar clasps, Bell caps and the "Mystery" clasp are things you may need to purchase, as well as #47 and #53 drill bits (for the "Mystery" clasps). In any case, these are necessary only for specific projects.

Multiple Twist

MULTIPLE STRANDS

Basically, all multiple strands are individually strung and then joined together onto one clasp: as twists, braids or bibs. Great effects can be accomplished with varying colors, textures, and sizes, or with uniformity. Necklaces can be finished to any length, although the weight of the beads must help determine how many strands are used.

Twisted Ribbons, Cords & Beads - Assorted Dangles
(Courtesy of Wendy Owen)

TWISTS AND BRAIDS
METHOD I

1) Layout the strands, (plain or knotted) leaving approximately 8 - 10" of thread at each end.

Lay out the strands.

2) Holding the ends of all strands together, twist or braid them together to make sure the finished length will be accurate.

3) Lay the strands out again.

4) Add or remove beads, according to need.

5) Tie another knot at the very end of each tail to keep the beads from sliding off.

6) Holding all the tails at one end together, make an overhand knot as close to the beads as possible. Glue the knot.

Make An Overhand Knot

7) Turn the work around and hold them by their opposite ends, so that the beads are tight against the knot made in step 5.

8) Gather all the strands together and twist,braid,or roll them into your design. Carefully holding the strands as tight as possible, knot the tails together with an overhand knot. Glue the knot.

Twist., then knot the tails together.

7

ALTERNATE CLOSURES
FOLDOVER CRIMP OR BEAD TIP

If the threads are thin and your end knot small enough, you may use a foldover crimp (without a hole) to hide the knot and to attach the clasp.

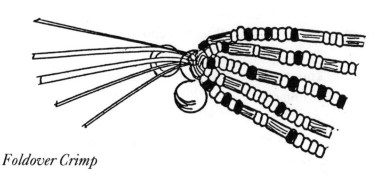

Foldover Crimp

BELLCAP OR CONE (CUPS)

Using an eyepin, make a firm and secure overhand knot through the eye. Glue the knot. Bring the pin through the wide end of the cap (or cone), and push the cap tight over the knot. Clip the excess cord and form a loop to attach the clasp.

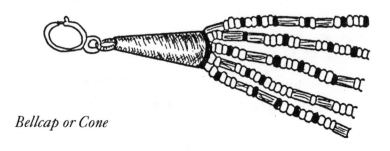

Bellcap or Cone

Make sure your clasp is sturdy enough to hold the weight and stress of the twist.

USING A MULTIPLE CLASP

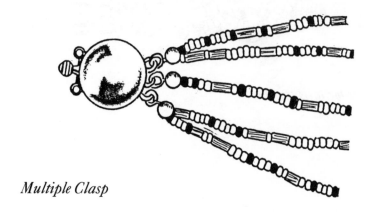

Multiple Clasp

1) Follow steps 1-5 as in Method I

2) Choose a multistrand clasp that provides enough loops and strength to hold all the strands. (You may attach 2-3 strands per loop, if practical.)

3) At one side, attach each strand to the clasp, using bead tips, foldover crimps, or French (bouillion) wire.

4) Twist, braid or roll all the strands into your design.

5) Attach each strand to the second side of the clasp, using the same closure as in Step 3.

GRADUATED OR "BIB" MULTISTRAND

Graduated Multistrand

This classic style has been popular for centuries, providing an elegant and flattering look to almost all beads. Any number of strands can be utilized, although size and weight are important considerations for wearability.

1) Choose the beads and multistrand clasp you want to use.

2) Lay out one strand at a time, starting with the longest.

3) String the longest strand, (plain or knotted) and attach it to the clasp, using crimps, beadtips or French bouillion wire.

4) Leaving 1/2" for very small beads, to 3" for very large beads, attach the second strand to the clasp. Try it on before you attach the second beadtip to see that the beads hang, without touching the lower strand.

5) Continue until all strands are attached to the clasp.

Simple, but luxurious!

THE DOG COLLAR

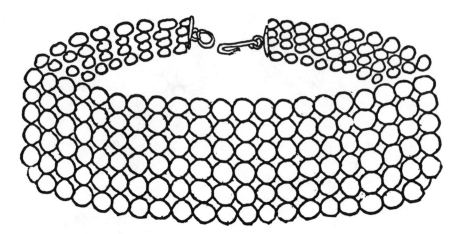

The Dog Collar

The true dog collar consists of at least three strands fitted closely to the neck. Since neck sizes vary greatly, the collar must be fitted to the individual, or constructed with a hook and chain adjustable closure.

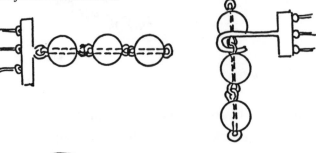

Hook & Chain Closure

1) Select the beads you wish to use keeping comfort size, weight and shape of beads in mind.

2) Layout each layer of beads to see how they look together. You may wish to use spacer bars to keep the beads aligned (eg: an 8mm 3 hole spacer will accommodate 3 strands of 8mm beads).

3) Thread or knot on your beads. Leave about 10" of excess thread at the end of each strand.

Spacer Bars

4) Attach one end of each strand to the hook end and the other end to the chain end, using crimps, beadtips or French bouillion wire.

5) Using a jump ring, attach a piece of chain approximately 2" long to the chain end. For a decorative touch, you may attach one bead to the end of the chain, using a headpin to attach the bead. The hook can be looped over any section of the chain to adjust the length.

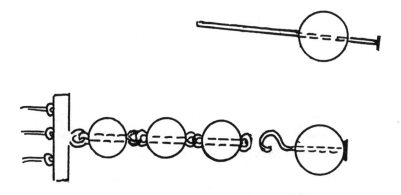

Add one bead to the chain.

6) Once you have mastered the adjustable dog collar, you might like to try the "fixed" fitted collar. It is imperative here to accurately measure the neck, as you may need to make each strand slightly longer than the one above it for proper fit. A beautifully crafted Victorian collar would be well worth the effort!

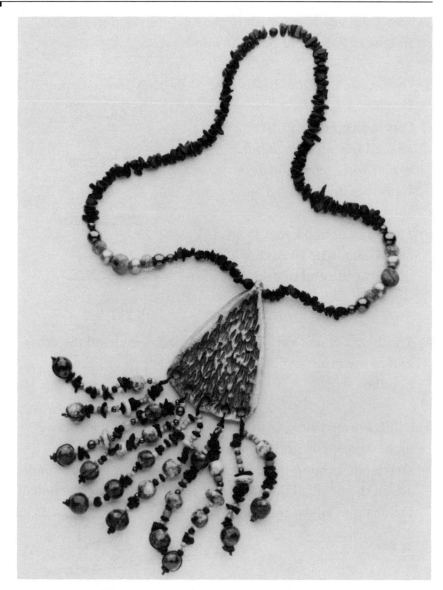

Porcelain Pendant & Beads, Black Onyx, Sterling

Designs can easily be enhanced by adding almost any object that captures your fancy. Wood, metal, stone, shell or clay placed in the center of a necklace, or strung between beads can be used to create very beautiful effects. Old coins, antique buckles, beaded tassels, or unusual found objects often bring ordinary beads into the realm of real works of art. Other techniques for tassels and pendants are described in Chapter VII "Using Wire & Chain"

The simplest pendant to attach is one with the bore hole drilled horizontally at the top.

Using tigertail, chain, or heavy cord, the necklace is started at the center, adding beads to each side. If the pendant has a front to back bore hole, a jump ring, splitring or bail may be used so that it lies flat.

Horizontal Bore Hole   *Pendant With Jump Ring*

Using Jump Rings For Pendants

Ivory Pendant With Cinnabar Beads
Knotted On Rattail

A simple, but attractive way to attach a pendant with cord,
(avoiding visible metal findings) is to thread on the pendant
using a macrame mounting or square knot,through the hole.

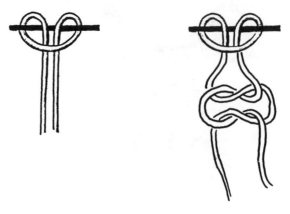

Mounting Knot   *Square Knot*

14

The option of using an accent bead to cover the knot is accomplished by threading both ends of the cord through the bead and pushing it down over the knot. This makes the knot more secure, as well as the pendant more interesting.

A very attractive and practical attachment can be made using small beads that blend with your design. Pass the cord through the bore hole, thread enough small beads on each side until you can form a loop around the top of the pendant. Tie a knot at the top of the loop

Bring the cords through a large bead and continue your design. Two or more loops can be used for effect, or for pendants with more than one hole.

METHOD III

Form a loop with small beads.

Sometimes oversized beads, or large (drilled through) flat pieces are desired for a central accent. To attach these with cord, thread down through the bead, through a second, small (bottom) bead and then back through the pendant.

METHOD IV

Thread down, then back up through the pendant.

15

TASSELS AND FRINGES

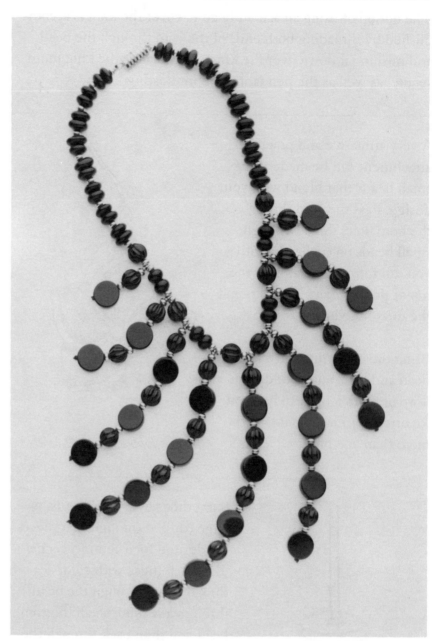

Black Onyx, Sterling Beads, Barrel Clasp

Small beads are generally used for tassels or fringe because they fall gracefully and add a decorative finishing touch to necklaces, earrings or pins. Made of short strands, tassels are usually gathered together at the top and connected through a large bead, or bellcap, and attached to the bottom of a necklace or the ends of a lariat or belt. Fringes are separate strands which add a graceful and dramatic touch to any design.

1) Decide how long, how full and what color the tassel will be. Lay out the beads.

2) Thread the needle, make a double knot at the end of the thread. Clip the ends and dab with glue.

3) Thread each tassel strand to the desired length, leaving 3" to 4" of cord at the top.

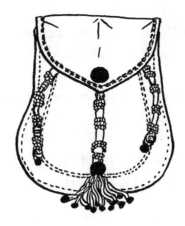

Tassels

4) Hold all the strands together and make a tight double overhand knot at the top, as close to the beads as possible. Clip the cords, Dab knot with glue.

Leave 3"-4" of cord.   *Make an overhand knot.*

5) Using a bell cap, or large holed bead, pull all the threads into the cap or bead. (The knot will be hidden inside.) If there are too many threads to pass through the main necklace beads, clip the extras, leaving 2,4, or 6 cords with which to work.

6) Continue stringing the necklace.

17

METHOD II

1) Follow steps 1-3.

2) Using an eyepin, tie each tassel strand securely to the eye loops. Clip the cord. Dab with glue.

5) Push the end of the eyepin through a bell cap (or large holed bead)

6) Clip the end of the eyepin leaving approximately one quarter (1/4") inch past the cap. Pull the bead tassel (tight) into the cap.

7) Using round nose pliers, bend the wire end into a circle.

8) Attach the tassel to your necklace, using any pendant attachment method.

METHOD III

1) Follow steps 1-3

4) Finish each tassel strand with a beadtip.

5) Attach all the beadtips to the eyepin.

6) Follow steps 5-8 of Method II

Finish each tassel with a beadtip.

The above can also be made using head pins, although the tassel will be stiff and not "flowing" as with cord. Attach all the head pins to the eyepin. Follow Steps 5-8 of METHOD II.

METHOD IV

FRINGES

Using fringe is another way of adding drama to necklaces, bracelets, pins, barrettes and earrings. A great variety of styles and methods utilize this skill and almost any combination of color and texture may be used. Usually a fringe of 2"-3" or longer will hang more gracefully. Beaded fringes may also be added to belts, handbags or clothing.

Several Fringe Styles

**METHOD I
USING BEADTIPS**

Mother Of Pearl, Sterling Beads, Barrel Clasp

19

1) Draw and/or layout your base necklace and fringe design.

2) String the base necklace and add clasp.

3) Thread the needle, using a double knot at the end of the thread. Dab knot with glue.

4) Thread each fringe to desired length, using a bead tip at the top.

Using a beadtip for fringe.

5) Starting your fringes at both sides of the center bead, attach the bead tip to the necklace in graduated lengths.

**METHOD II
USING DOUBLE THREAD**

1) Draw and/or layout your design, deciding where the fringes will be, and if they will be graduated in size and length.

2) String the base necklace leaving 5"-6" of cord at each end. Tape or knot the thread ends to secure the beads.

3) Find the necklace center and appropriate fringe placement. (leave at least one bead between each fringe).

4) Using a second cord, string through the base necklace until the first fringe point is reached.

5) Attach the fringe by threading down through the (fringe) beads, through the bottom bead, then back up through the (fringe) beads again.

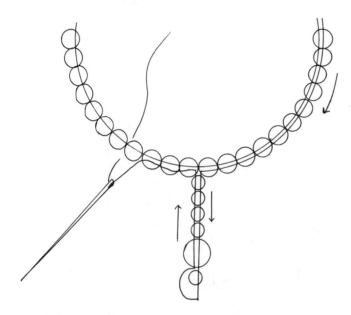

Using a second cord for fringe.

6) Make a secure knot at the top, connecting the fringe to the base.

7) Continue on through the necklace.

8) When all the fringes have been added, finish the necklace ends.

---

1) Measure and layout the necklace.

**METHOD III
MACRAME KNOT**

2) Starting at both sides of the center bead, attach the fringe cord by using a lark's head or mounting knot. Since these cords are doubled, make sure they are thin enough to pass through the beads twice.

3) Thread down through the fringe beads, then back up, securing each to the base necklace with a knot. NOTE: An alternate to Step 3 is to thread down through the fringe beads, tie a secure knot and dab the knot with glue.

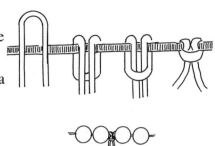

Mounting Or Lark's Head Knot

METHOD IV
LOOPED FRINGE

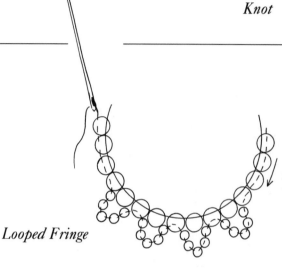

Looped Fringe

1) Follow METHOD I/ Steps 1-4

5) Thread cord through the base necklace, through beads for the loop, then back into the necklace. Skip one or more beads (for spacers) between each loop.

6) Continue to the end of the necklace.

LARIATS

High drama and/or great effects can be achieved by wrapping long strands of beads around the neck, or tying them, leaving fancy ends to dangle gracefully. Standard lariats are 48" or longer, but the lariat can be made just long enough to make a simple overlapping knot or clip at the front. Tassels, fringes or one fancy bead can be used at the ends.

Lariat

1) Determine the length by loosely wrapping or tying cord around the neck.

2) Layout beads. Measure the cord.

3) Thread the needle and double knot the cord. Glue knot. Attach bead tip.

4) Thread on beads until the desired length is reached.

5) Attach the 2nd bead tip.

Attach beadtips to each end.

6) A tassel or bead can now be attached to the bead tips.

The lariat ends can be finished using any of the previously described methods for adding a tassel.

THE MYSTERY CLASP
(WITH PEARLS)

Now you see it, now you don't.

Although pearls have to be drilled to fit this clasp, the effort is well worth it! Since the clasp is invisible, beads can be arranged in very interesting combinations....singles, doubled, or joined for opera length. Generally, cultured pearls are used, but if using stone beads, it is advisable to have a professional lapidary do the drilling (Refer to Chapter VIII for drilling instructions).

1) Measure the millimeter size of both sides of the clasp; the "female" end and "male" end.

Mystery Clasp

2) Generally size #47 and #53 (for standard 14K clasps) are used to drill two beads. Make sure the clasp fits each drill hole.

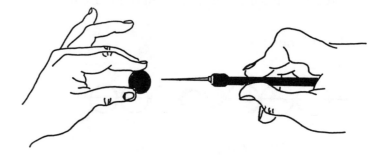

Pearls must be drilled to fit the clasp.

3) Set clasp aside

4) Measure cord for knotting half of the pearls. Double knot the end. Dab with glue. Set half the strand aside.

5) Thread cord through the drilled female bead. Pull tight so knot is inside. Knot half of the beads.

Pull cord through the drilled female bead.

6) Thread cord through the male end bead. Knot the rest of the beads.

7 Join the pearls at center of strand (as if you're knotting continuously).

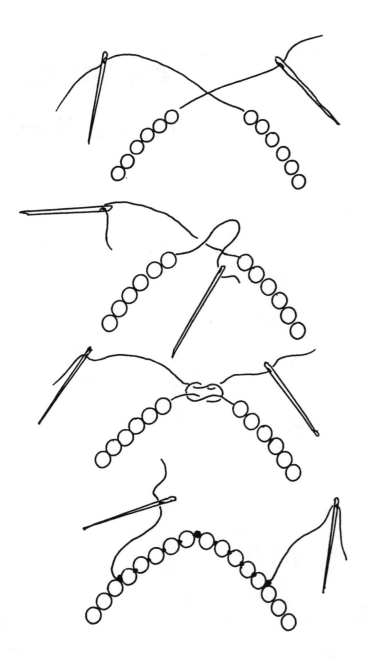

Join pearls at center of strand.

8) Using cyranacyclate or epoxy, glue each clasp end into the proper hole.

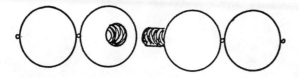

Glue each section into the proper hole.

Finis! The clasp will screw together invisibly! A 25" necklace plus 7" bracelet makes a 32" necklace when two clasps are attached.

CHAPTER III

Off Loom Weaving

Antique Beads with Smokey Quartz Drops by Susan Hoge, The Bead Gallery

It is not surprising that such a profusion of names exists to describe identical bead-weaving techniques. Almost every group in the world, from the most primitive to the most sophisticated, has used these methods at some period of time in history. Whatever we call them, whatever materials, or designs are employed, beautiful art can result from weaving beads. Each section of this chapter deals with a different technique. Starting with single thread weaving and progressing to more complicated procedures, you'll discover how simple they are, once your fingers have mastered the technique. Everything in this chapter and more is possible with time and practice.

OFF LOOM WEAVING
EQUIPMENT

A fine, sharp scissor, beeswax to strengthen cord, crystal cement or glue, a tape measure and chain nose plier are necessities. For storing your beads, anything from plastic boxes to zip lock bags, can be used, although these are not efficient for the actual work. Shallow saucers or small coasters work well, as tiny beads can be kept apart and easily picked up onto the needle.

A simple work table can be constructed from 1" thick styrofoam or wood approximately 18" square, and covered with smooth fabric. A commercial macrame board also works very well. Use corsage or tee pins to fasten your work. An assortment of small drills or broaches are handy to enlarge bead holes when necessary.

MATERIALS

Since most bead weaving requires the needle and thread to pass through the beads more than once, you'll need needles in fine and medium sizes plus a selection of threads. Trial and error work best, as there is no perfect thread or needle. If suitable, some designs may be worked with monofiliment nylon or fine wire.

MISCELLANEOUS

All designs may be drawn on graph paper with crayons or felt markers. If you are new to this kind of stringing, choose large beads and easy projects to begin. Whatever beads you choose, remember that cheap materials produce cheap results.

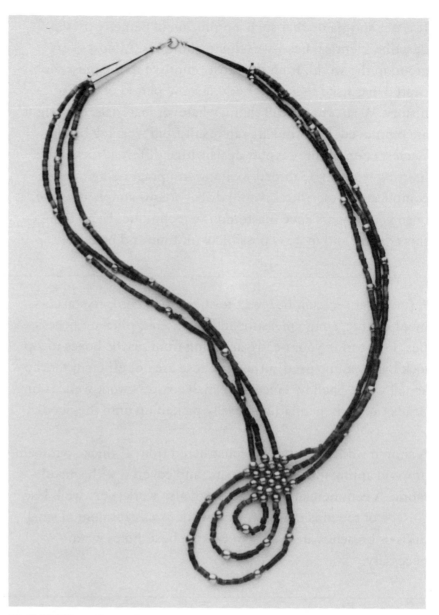

Shell & Silver Cross-Over Fringe
(Courtesy of Wendy Owen)

GENERAL DIRECTIONS

1) Before you begin, organize your beads according to size and color. Be sure you have more than enough to finish the project.

2) Always test needle and thread before you start.

3) Some beads have sharp or poorly drilled holes. Discard them as you work, as they may fray or tear the thread.

4) Wax the thread periodically to keep it slick and strong.

5) To add or tie off threads, leave enough tail to knot, glue and run the (old) thread back about 1 inch through the beads.

6) For clarity, the diagrams show wide spaces between each bead. In actual practice, tension should be tight enough so that almost no thread shows.

7) The following procedures are worked with one needle and may be used to make simple or complex articles to wear, or decorate the house. Each technique lends itself to many applications. Practice, experiment with beads and color and use your imagination!

BASIC WEAVING
METHOD I

1) Select any beads of uniform size, with holes large enough for the thread to pass through twice. Beads may be round or cylindrical.

2) Use a Nylon Needle Card, or thread 2 yards of nylon onto a needle.
Test to make sure the needle and thread pass through the holes twice.

Thread nylon onto needle.

3) Make a double knot at the end of the thread.

4) String on 15 beads.

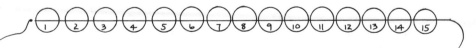

5) Push the needle and thread back through bead #14. Pull the thread tight.

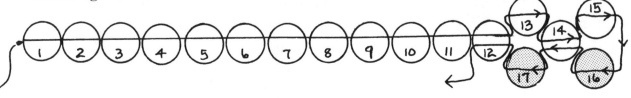

29

6) Thread on another bead. Go back through bead #13. Pull the thread tight.

7) Continue adding one bead at a time, (pulling the thread tight each time), until the end of the row. (bead #1)

8) Thread on another bead. (bead #16)

9) Now moving from right to left, go back through bead #3.

10) Continue. Note that each bead will fit snugly between the 2 beads in the previous row.

11) When your practice workpiece looks smooth and uniform, try different colors in alternating rows.

12) To finish off, thread back through three beads, knot, go back three more beads, knot again, dab a bit of glue on the thread, go back three more beads and clip the thread.

BASIC WEAVING METHOD II

This stitch is exactly like METHOD I, but picks up and strings two beads instead of one. Try it! The same basic weave creates a totally different effect!

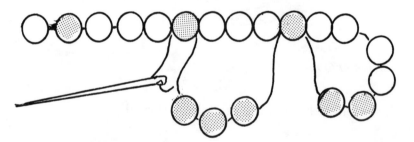

String 2 or more beads.

For a lacy look, pick up and string three beads, four, five or more! The technique is the same, row by row. The results are amazingly different!

Key Ring on Leather Core

This stitch is most commonly known as the "Peyote" or "Gourd" stitch. Exactly like METHOD I weaving, it is worked around a central core, bead by bead, forming a spiral pattern. Sometimes the beads are placed permanently onto the core (eg: nylon rope or heavy cord) and sometimes an open cylinder is formed by utilizing a temporary support (eg: a dowel or pencil) and removing it when the piece is finished. Nylon thread is recommended for this stitch, although some people prefer monofiliment.

WEAVING ONTO A CORE

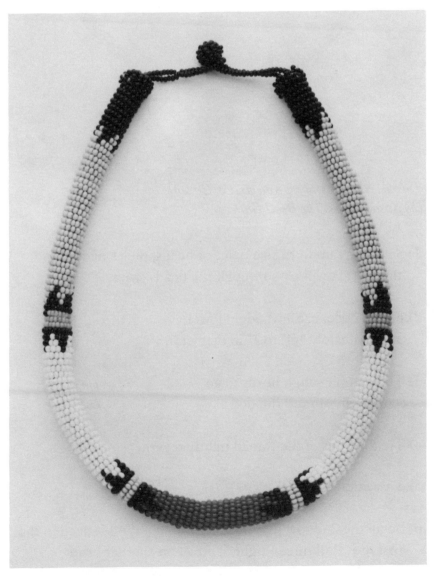

Gourd Stitch with Button Loop Closure

Torque: Silver, Amber, Amethyst & Crystal
(by Susan Hoge, The Bead Gallery)

1) Select any uniform size practice beads, plus a needle and thread that will pass through the beads twice.

2) For practice, use a wooden dowel approximately 1/4" to 1" in diameter.

3) Thread on enough beads to go completely around the dowel.

1/4" to 1"
Diameter

4) Tie the ends of the thread tightly together.

5) Thread on a bead.

6) Begin the 2nd row by threading through the 1st bead in the first row. Pull thread tight. Thread on another bead.

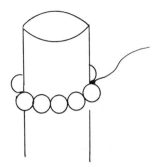

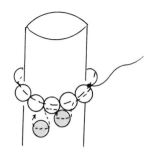

Tie the ends of the thread tightly.   *The second row.*

7) Thread on another bead.

8) Go through the 3rd bead (in first row). Pull thread tight.

9) Continue until the 2nd row is completed. Pull thread tight.

10) Thread on a bead.

11) Go through the 1st bead in the 2nd row. Pull thread tight.

12) Continue working rows, one bead at a time.

13) Finish off as in Method I.

Gourd Stitch on Permanent Core

The peyote or gourd stitch is very effective for permanently covering a round or irregular object with beads. This type of beading requires beads of uniform size. For flexible necklaces, belts and bracelets the center core is generally soft rope, cords or leather strands.

PERMANENT CORE

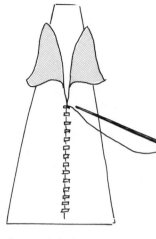

For solid objects such as metal or wood bracelets, combs and jars, or other artwork, fabric or thin leather is fitted and sewn over the solid core. A few drops of glue may be used to secure the fabric cover.

To work the peyote stitch on a permanent core, some craftspeople stitch the beads onto the backing for added strength. If the tension is properly done, this is not required.

Leather or fabric sewn onto the core.

THE BRICK STITCH

This stitch gets its name from it's "brick-like" appearance as well as its strength. Since it never needs fabric backing, it is often found in intricate earring and necklace designs. Obviously, threads going back through each bead several times, make the finished piece quite firm and secure. The stitch can be done going across the beads, or when adding fringes stitched in vertical lengths.

Seed Bead Earrings: Brick & Flower Variation with Fringe

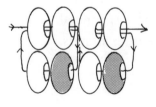
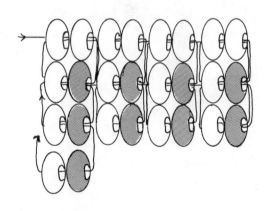

Horizontal Brick Stitch (Going Back Two Beads)

34

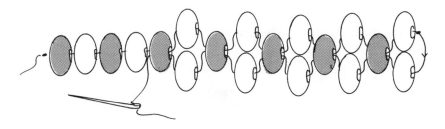

Twill Stitch (One Bead at a Time)

The "V" formed by this stitch can be narrow or wide, delicate or large, colorful or conservative. Very attractive for collars, belts and bracelets, the dimensions can easily be changed. Alter the chevron by changing the bead proportions to four and five, five and six, seven and eight, etc., or by using oval or tubed beads for the "V" stations.

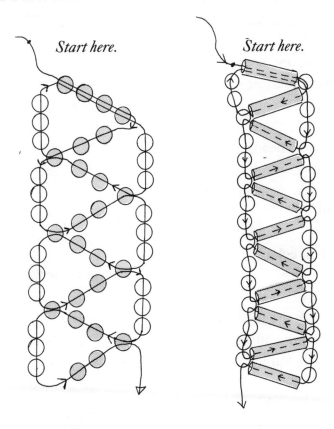

Start here.   *Start here.*

Chevron Stitch   *Chevron Using Tube Beads*

A great variety of designs are possible with this very simple, but effective technique. Woven into necklaces, bracelets, rings or hanging pendants and earrings, the possibilities seem endless. Try the stitch with all sizes and colors of beads, with single or continuous "chains" and with uniform "daisies" or unique flowers with mysteriously large centers.

The Flower Chain

Nylon thread is recommended for strength, but chokers, bracelets and rings may be constructed with elastic. Here too, the thread must pass through some beads more than once, so test before you begin.

1) Using doubled thread, cut to desired length. Wax the thread.

2) Thread on one bead and secure it with a knot. Leave about 8" of thread at the end.

Thread on 8 beads.

3) Thread on 8 beads color (A)

4) Go back through the first color (A) bead.

5) Thread on color (B) (center) bead.

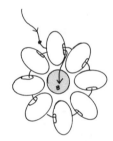

Thread on the 9th bead.

6) Go through the fifth color (A) bead. Pull thread tight. The "flower" is formed.

7) Thread on 8 color (A) beads.

8) Repeat the pattern.

Go through the 5th bead.

Experiment with different sizes, shapes and colors, and with varying numbers of "petal" or "loop" beads. To make a continuous chain, the petals are connected to each other, with no color (A) spacers.

Woven Lace Collar
Black Seed Beads with Button-Loop Closure

This wonderful pattern is known as "Mexican Lace", "Honey-comb Lace", "Zigzag Lace", "Contour Lace", "Greenland Netting", plain "Netting" and "Vandyke Lace",(named after the 17th century painter whose portraits frequently included zigzag collars.) It is an elegant technique, providing a way to make collars, cuffs, handbags and many other "Lace" accessories.

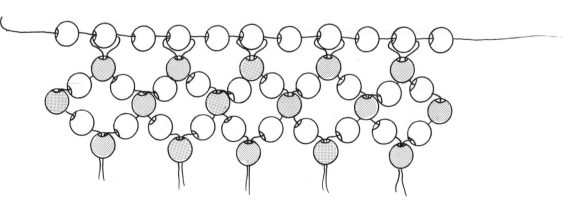

Vertical Lace

37

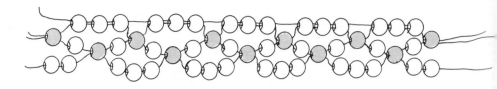

Horizontal Lace

Essentially a simple procedure, it may be worked vertically or horizontally. By increasing the number of beads in each row, intricate contoured collars emerge.

Strong nylon thread or monofiliment nylon should be used, with different colors and sizes of beads for totally different effects. Practice first with simple two color strips, then a bracelet or choker, and finally, when comfortable with the technique, try a contoured collar. With some practice, you'll find your own unique applications for this beadwork.

HORIZONTAL LACE

1) Measure and cut approximately 3 yards of nylon. Make a double knot at the end.

2) Working with 2 bead colors, Thread on 2 light, 1 dark. 3 light, 1 dark, etc. until 17 beads are strung.

3 Start the second row with 2 dark beads. Go through the 3rd bead (dark). Pull thread tight. String 3 light beads. Go through the next dark bead. Pull tight. Continue to end of row.

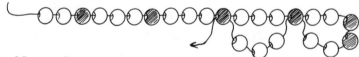

Horizontal Lace - Steps 1-3

4) String the 3rd and 4th rows following the diagrams.

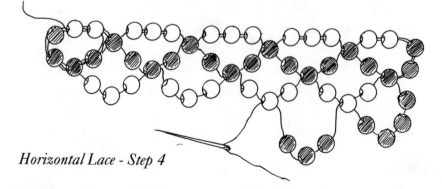

Horizontal Lace - Step 4

After you've completed 7 or 8 rows, experiment with different beads and patterns, eg. use 5 light beads and go through 1 dark, or 6 light beads and go through 2 dark. There are so many variations possible, the only way to learn is to experiment.

Vertical Lace Collar

The Vertical Pattern is really easy, once you've tried it with success. It looks very complicated, but if you practice with contrasting beads and the three and one pattern, you'll begin to see the "diamond" shape emerge.

1) Measure and cut approximately 3 yards of nylon. Make a double knot at end.

2) Thread on 1 dark, 3 light, 1 dark, 3 light, until you have 21 beads.

3) At the end of the row, thread on 3 light, and pass back through the first dark bead. Pull thread tight.

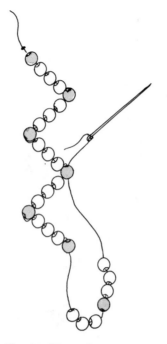

4) Continue pattern, going through every other dark bead, (every 8 beads), turning at the end of each row.

5) Experiment with different patterns until you feel secure.

NOTE: To construct a contoured collar, more beads must be progressively added at the bottom of the piece. The more beads you add, the larger the "diamonds" become. Practice and experiment with round, oval or square beads and different colors. The results will amaze you!

Vertical Lace Steps 1-5

DOUBLE THREAD WEAVING

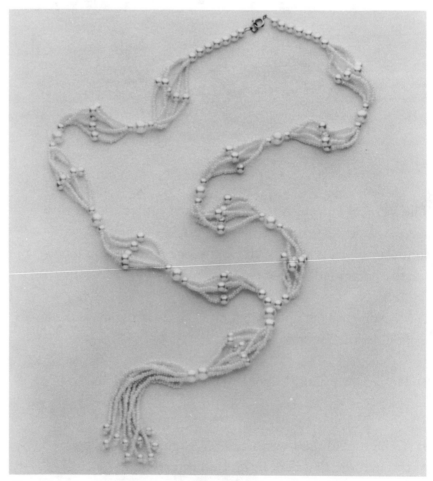

Parallel Weaving with Tassel, Faux Pearls

40

Two basic techniques are demonstrated in this section, both employing two or more threads. Often adapted for large projects such as belts and bags, their use in designing uniquely attractive bracelets, necklaces and rings is unlimited.

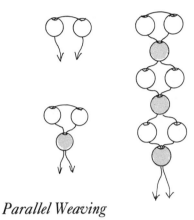

Parallel Weaving

Parallel Weaving is also known as Double-needle, Two-thread and Double-end weaving. It is worked with two independent threads strung through two beads, then passed together through a central core. All the beads face the same (parallel) direction.

PARALLEL WEAVING

Cross-needle, Cross-over, or Cross-threading also employs two independent threads, passing through a central core, but in this technique the threads cross each other in opposite directions. The core or center will lay sideways, (or horizontally) in the pattern. These basic methods are the basis for unlimited design variations. Practice some of the following patterns with different colors, sizes and shapes.

CROSS-NEEDLE

Cross-needle Weaving

PARALLEL WEAVING
VARIATIONS

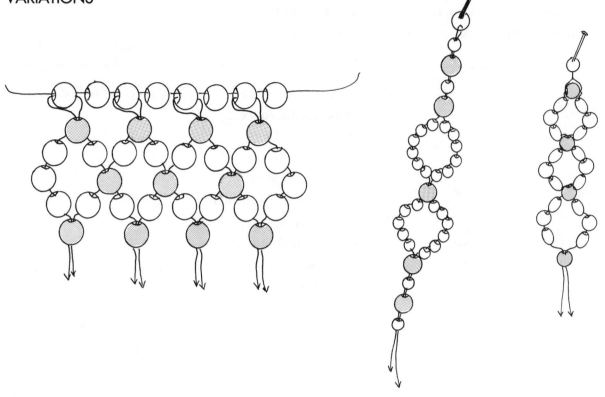

CROSS-NEEDLE
VARIATIONS

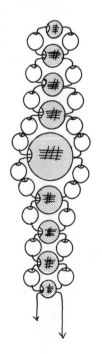
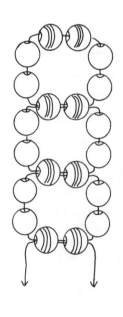
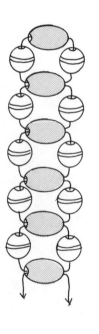
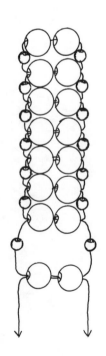

42

1) All Work using the 2 cord technique should be fastened to a secure work surface.

*Work Surface
(Board with Nail)*

2) Single threads, doubled threads, wire, monofiliment nylon and elastic may be used with or without needles. The thread must be thin enough to pass through the core beads more than once.

3) Tighten the threads gently as you work so that the design lays flat and remains flexible.

4) Before you begin, be sure you have sufficient beads for your whole project.

5) Since the thread will be visible with crossover techniques, its color is quite important. If possible, use matching thread, a decorative contrast, or colorless monofiliment nylon.

MULTIPLE CORDS

This technique is particularly effective for "fabrics" made entirely of beads. Practice with large beads and fairly thin cord until you've mastered the process.

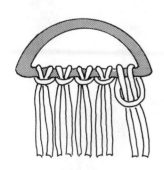

Fasten the cords with mounting knots.

1) Using 5 double threads attach them to a belt buckle, or large split ring with macrame mounting knots. Fasten the end to a working surface.

2) Thread on 5 beads. (Through each doubled cord)

3) Thread on 2 more rows of 5 beads.

43

4) Separate the cords. Thread 1 bead on cord 1.

5) Thread another bead on cord 1 and 2.

6) Thread the 3rd bead on cord 2 and 3.

7) Follow the (dark) cords in diagram.

8) Continue, separating the cords every third row.

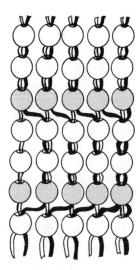

Multiple cords using parallel pattern.

CLOSURES

Button & loop closure.

To make a "button-loop" closure, finish off one end of the necklace with a well-secured large bead (or button), and the other end with a series of small beads, threaded to form a loop. Pass the thread through the loop beads twice and secure it by threading back through several inches of the necklace.

Many commercial clasps are suitable for woven bracelets and necklaces. The weight and design of the finished piece should always be considered.

Parallel stringing.

*Necklace, Horn, Bone,
Bamboo & Leather
(Courtesy of Wendy Owen)*

TOP
*Antique Glass, Smokey
Quartz Drops
(by Susan Hoge,
The Bead Gallery)*

BOTTOM
*Choker, Inlaid Turquoise
and Silver, Hematite Beads*

OPPOSITE
*42" Chain Necklace, Glass
Beads & Cabachon
(Mirium Haskell)*

COLOR PLATES

TOP
*Beaded Bag, Faux Pearls
and Silk
(Courtesy of Gertrude
Freedman)*

BOTTOM
*Gourd Stitch; Antique
Bracelet, Choker, Sculpture;
West Africa*

OPPOSITE
*Antique Yoruba Necklace
(Courtesy of Patricia
Woodbury)*

COLOR PLATES

TOP
Necklace, Wood, Horn,
Ceramic & Brass
(Courtesy of Wendy Owen)

MIDDLE
Bracelet, Carnelian, Jade,
Amethyst Lapiz & Quartz
with Silver Wire

BOTTOM
Antique Glass and
Fresh Water Pearls
(by Susan Hoge, The Bead
Gallery, Ann Arbor

OPPOSITE
Antique Silver Pendant with
Silver Beads; Ethiopia

*Necklace, Gourd Stitch
with Fringe
(Courtesy of
The Bead Gallery)*

CHAPTER IV

Loom Weaving

LOOM
Frame or machine for weaving fabric with thread or yarn.

WARP
The threads fastened lengthwise in the loom.

WEFT
The side to side threads which interlace across the warp.

According to archeologists, the art of weaving was already known when primitive man made mats and baskets by intertwining various materials. The remains of woven textiles found in Egypt indicate that it had become a sophisticated craft by the 15th Century B.C. Using porcupine quills for centuries before Europeans introduced glass beads, American Indians perpetuated their extraordinary designs through the art of woven beadwork.

Weaving beads on a loom creates a beaded "fabric", with only the beads showing. Since the basic technique is fairly simple and the results so gratifying, it's not surprising that this historic artform has sustained its popularity for so long.

Many inexpensive, commercial looms are available through craft supply stores. Made of metal, wood or rigid plastic, with adjustable rollers, they are a good starting point for simple designs and small-scale work.

Wood Loom

After some experience, you may want to construct your own loom, designed for a specific project. Since its purpose is simply to support the warp threads, it can easily be made with some scrap wood and nails. Three effective designs are illustrated.

#1) Use 3/4" to 1" thick wood, about 5" to 6" wide. Make base (length) 3" to 5" longer than needed. Make end pieces 3" to 5" high. Use common nails or cuphooks to hold the warp threads taut.

THREE DESIGNS

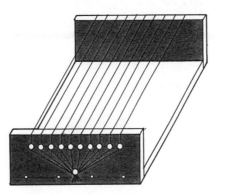

Loom #1

#2) Use 4 side pieces 3" to 5" high. Use two 1/4" bolts 2" longer than width. Use two nuts to fit bolts. Use two 1 1/2" common nails.

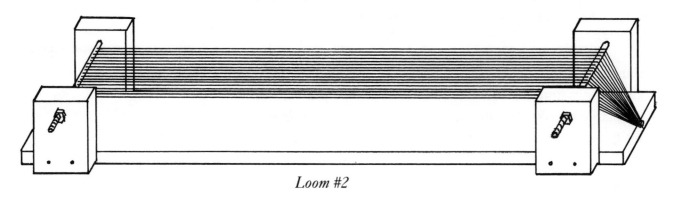

Loom #2

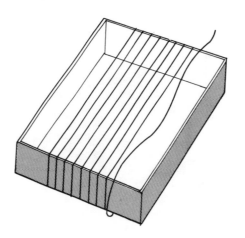

Loom #3

#3) A box loom can be made from a square or rectangular picture frame or 4 pieces of sturdy wood nailed together.

NOTE: Some looms are made with notches or combs to separate the warp threads. If the warp is properly strung, these are not needed; the first row of beads will keep them evenly spaced.

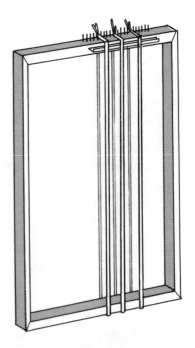

Picture Frame Loom

Bead needle sizes vary according to their origin. English needles are generally matched to bead sizes: #10 for #10 beads, size #12 for #12 beads. To simplify the confusion, have a selection of needles on hand ranging from #10 to #16. (The lower the number, the thicker the needle.)

NEEDLES

Strong crochet cotton #30 is suggested for the loom (or warp) threads as it does not stretch. The weft (or beading) thread should be nylon, pre-tested to be sure it can pass through the bead holes two or three times. The weft thread can be single or doubled.

THREAD

You should have a pair of chain pliers, graph paper, crayons or color pencils for designing, a ruler or tape measure, and of course, some sharp scissors. A cake of beeswax is recommended to strengthen the warp threads.

MISCELLANEOUS

The most popular beads for loom work are "Seed Beads", ranging in size from the largest #9, to the smallest #16. In truth, almost any size or shape beads can be used, so long as they are uniform. Too large a hole or one slightly different size bead can spoil a whole piece! Check their size as you go along, discarding any that are uneven.

BEADS

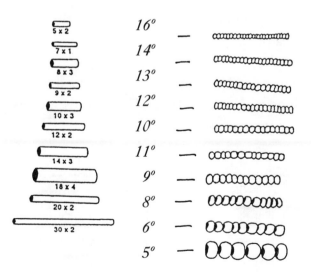

Approximate Beads per Inch

If this is your first loom project, use larger beads to start with, preferably "pony beads" size #7 to #9. They have bigger holes and the work will progress quickly.

GENERAL DIRECTIONS

1) Be sure you have more than enough beads for the whole project.

2) In charted designs, each vertical line equals one warp thread.

3) Work on a white cloth or piece of felt, to prevent the beads from rolling. Your beads can also be spread out on this cloth and easily seen and picked up onto the needle.

4) Be absolutely sure that the warp threads are long enough for your piece.

5) Both warp and weft threads should be rubbed with beeswax.

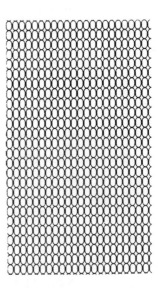

Loom Paper

6) Push each row of beads up close, with no spaces left between rows.

7) To make a bracelet or headband, round elastic thread can be used for the warp.

8) Inventive designs can be created with large wood or glass beads combined with thick warp and weft cords such as rat-tail, embroidery yarns and jute.

 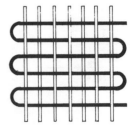

Basic Weaves

1) The best loom thread is crochet cotton, since nylon tends to stretch.

2) Since the beads lie between each loom thread, you'll always need one thread more than the number of beads.

3) Carefully check the design to see how many warp threads are needed.

4) For strength, use doubled thread at the two outer edges of the warp.

5) To string the loom, tie the end of the cotton to the nail on the side of the loom. Going back and forth across the top of the loom, wrap the thread securely around each nail until you have the required number of warp threads. The threads should be taut and straight.

6) Tie the last thread onto a nail securely and cut.

7) Rub beeswax across the warp.

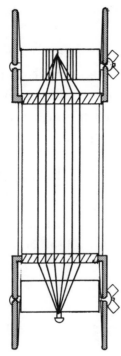

Six warp threads strung for five beads.

LOOM WEAVING

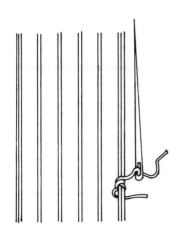

Tie the thread to the weft.

1) Using strong nylon, thread about 2 feet of waxed thread. Leave a tail approximately 10 inches long.

2) Test the thread to be sure it will go through the beads twice.

3) Measure 2" from the end of the loom and tie the thread to one of the outside weft threads. (Leave a tail about 3" long).

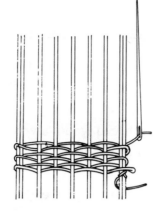

Weave 5 rows for firm top.

4) Without any beads, weave 5 rows over and under the warp, this creates a firm top and insures that the beadwork will not unravel when removed from the loom.

5) Thread on the beads you need for the first row, and slide them down to the end.

6) Pass these strung beads under the loom threads and press them up with your fingers so that each bead lies between a warp thread.

7) Now holding the beads up in place, pass the needle (over the warp) back through the beads. Pull thread tight.

8) Repeat steps 5 - 7.

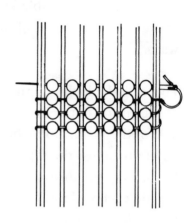

Pass the needle through the beads.

Break unwanted bead with pliers.

9) If you accidentally put on an extra bead, the unwanted bead should be broken off with a chain or flat plier. Protect your eyes, place the plier against the bead holes and break the bead.

ADDING ON THREAD
METHOD I

When the beading (weft) thread has about 4" - 5" left, you'll need to add more thread.

1) Re-weave the old thread back through 2 finished rows of beads. Clip off any tail.

2) Re-thread the needle, and tie the end of the thread to an outside (warp) thread. (Leave the tails. These are picked up later and woven back through the beads).

3) Continue weaving.

1) Re-weave the old thread back through 2 finished rows. Leave a tail.

2) Re-thread the needle. Go back 3 finished rows and tie the new thread to a middle warp thread. Leave a tail.

3) Now pass the new thread through the finished rows (again) to the start of a new row.

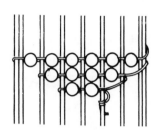

4) Clip the tails close to the beads and dab with glue.

5) Continue weaving.

To decrease beads.

NOTE: You may find that a smaller needle is needed to do the re-weaving.

FINISHING OFF
METHOD I

When the last beaded row is done, repeat what you did at the beginning: Weave 5 rows without beads back and forth across the loom threads. Knot the bead thread to the warp.

1) Before removing your work, use adhesive or masking tape to make a "sandwich" all around the warp threads. Press the tape firmly, close to the last row of beads.

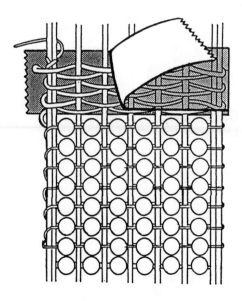

Use tape to make a sandwich.

2) When both ends are
   taped, cut the warp
   threads from the
   loom, leaving at
   least 2"-3" of thread.

3) Knot the warp
   threads in pairs.

4) Fold the ends back
   under the design
   and stitch in place.

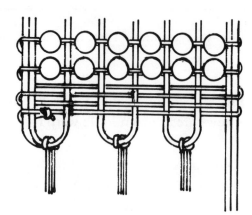

Knot the warp threads.

5) Sew a fabric or soft leather backing at both ends of the
   weaving. A closure may be sewn to this backing, or the fabric
   can be a long enough piece to use as a tie.

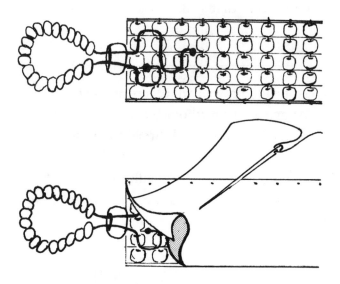

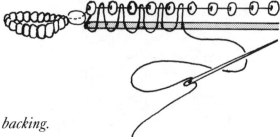

Sewing on a backing.

The piece may also be lined with a length of fabric stitched to
the whole weaving.

Combs

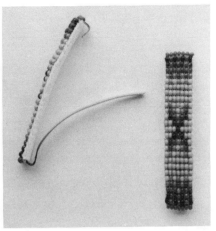

Barrettes

1) Cut the weaving thread at least 5" away from the beads.

2) Pair off the warp threads and knot them with a square knot.

3) Threading one warp thread at a time, weave back through one or two rows.

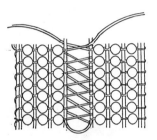

To join ends, weave back and forth.

4) Trim off the tails.

METHOD II

NOTE: Since there are so many techniques and no set rules, one should always be willing to experiment! Mix beading techniques; add fringes and tassels; try shells, wood, ceramic, and metal beads. Work freely without a pattern. Make a great size loom and create a beaded wall hanging! In short, have fun!

CHAPTER V

Bead Embroidery

*Embroidered Bag
(Courtesy of
Gertrude Freedman)*

When beads are sewn directly onto material of any kind, the result is called embroidery or needlepoint. Finished sections of embroidered fabric stitched onto a separate backing is termed applique, overlay, or applied work. Since their ancient origins, many different names have accumulated to describe a few techniques, but essentially there are really only three basic methods.

The most popular procedure, called "Lazy Stitch" uses a single thread to attach a small number of beads with each stitch. The second, called "Couching", uses two threads. The third and simplest style is "Scatter Beading" and entails sewing on one bead at a time. One other section in this chapter covers the "Tambour Shuttle", a tool still in use for rapid production of beaded clothing and accessories.

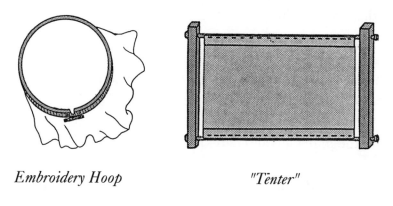

Embroidery Hoop   *"Tenter"*

EQUIPMENT AND SUPPLIES

Regardless of the method employed, some kind of frame is necessary to keep the fabric taut and prevent puckering. A commercial embroidery hoop made of wood or plastic works effectively. Another functional, and simple frame ("Tenter") can be constructed from one inch wood strips or an artist's stretcher frame. Four strips are cut so that they fit together rigidly. The fabric can then be tacked to the frame.

SCATTER STITCH

Variously called "Scatter Stitch", "Single Stitch" or "Tacking Stitch", the technique of adding one bead at a time can be time consuming, but very effective. Individually placed beads can create wonderful highlights, or bright spots of color. Exciting patterns may be developed by combining plain embroidery with scattered beads, sequins or buttons.

1) Place the fabric in the embroidery hoop or tack it to a frame.

Mark your design.

2) Mark your design with chalk or light pencil dots. If you're experienced, draw your design directly on the fabric. If this is your first try, choose a simple pattern and apply it to the fabric using iron-on or paper transfers. with a tracing wheel (found in fabric stores).

Tracing Wheel

3) Thread the needle with about a yard of nylon thread as heavy as the beads and fabric will permit.

4) Knot the end. Clip and dab knot with glue.

5) Pass the needle up through the fabric in place where bead is to go.

6) Thread a bead onto the needle and down to the fabric.

7) Insert needle back into fabric right next to the bead.

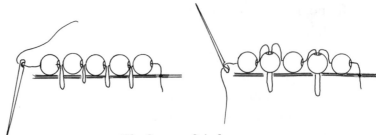

The Scatter Stitch.

8) Bring the needle up in position for the next bead and continue.

Yoruba Necklace
Courtesy Patricia Woodbury, The Bead Gallery

1-6) Follow steps one through six above.

BACK STITCH

7) Bring the needle back up to the right of the bead, go back
   through the bead, then back down through the fabric.
   Continue with one backstitch per bead.

Backstitch 1 bead.   *Backstitch 3 beads.*

LAZY STITCH

Using the "Lazy" or "Lazy Squaw" Stitch is the most popular, efficient and attractive way to decorate cloth or leather in the shortest amount of time. Since three or more beads are placed with each stitch, the fabric can quickly be densely covered in straight lines, curves or circles. The number of beads worked depends upon their size and the strength of the fabric. Curves and circles are easier to control with only 2 or 3 beads at a time.

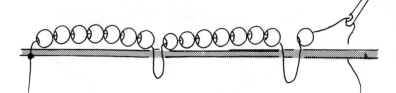

Lazy Stitch

Use good strong nylon thread as the bead bore holes may wear away cotton or linen. Be sure to have enough beads to complete the project, as different dye lots frequently vary in both color and size. Many bead workers prefer to complete the design and then applique it to a different backing of fabric.

LAZY SQUAW STITCH

This is almost exactly like the LAZY STITCH. Several beads are strung on and stitched to the base fabric but only at the end of the row. The thread is then brought down to the next row and the direction is reversed.

NOTE: Since the LAZY STITCH is much like a running stitch, its great dis-advantage is its lack of stability and strength. To solve this problem, as well as to make the thread almost invisible, backstitch through the last bead in every run.

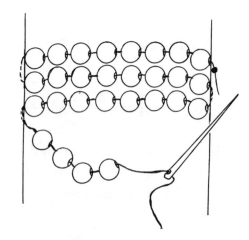

Lazy Squaw Stitch

The word "Couching" comes from the French "Coucher" which means, "to lie down." Sometimes called "Spot" or "Overlay" stitch, this technique requires 2 threaded needles. The first thread carries and lays down the beads, the second thread anchors them.

Follow steps 1-5 of the Scatter Stitch.

6) Thread on required numbers of beads, and lay them onto the cloth to fit your design. A thicker thread may be used for the beading thread as it does not pass through the fabric.

Fringed Seed Beads
Courtesy Wendy Owens

7) Thread the second needle. Knot, clip and dab with glue.

8) Push the second needle up through the cloth between two beads and make a stitch over the beaded thread, then back down to the underside.

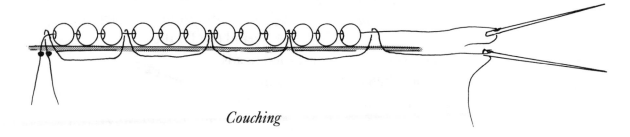

Couching

9) Repeat this procedure, with the beading thread on top and the "couching" thread underneath. NOTE: the number of couched stitches utilized depends totally upon the design. For tight curving lines and circles, more stitches and smaller beads may be needed. Practicing your pattern on scrap fabric is recommended!

TO FINISH OFF

Sew down through the fabric, up through the last bead and double back through 2 or 3 beads. On the underside, double knot the thread, clip and dab the knot with glue.

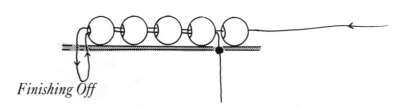

Finishing Off

TAMBOURING

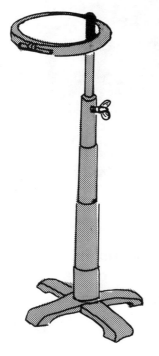

Tambour (Hoop) on Stand

Very popular during the 18th Century and again during the 1920's, tambouring is executed with loosely woven muslin, or fine lacy fabrics stretched onto a tambour (hoop or frame). The tambour hook (or shuttle) works by pulling the thread through the fabric into a continuous chain stitch. Resembling a very fine, sharp crochet hook, the tambour shuttle is set into a hollow wood, bone or steel handle, generally containing spare hooks inside. Hooks are interchangeable. When using beads, the design must be worked from the back of the fabric, with one hand controlling the hook (above the frame) and the other hand (under the frame) guiding the threaded beads. Chain stitch embroidery done in India with an "ari" is very similar.

Tambour Shuttle (Hook)

1) Stretch the fabric WRONG SIDE UP onto an embroidery hoop or frame.

2) Thread approximately 36" of beads onto good, strong nylon, directly from the spool. DO NOT CUT THE THREAD.

3) Using a pin, anchor the last bead to the fabric under the frame, at the right side. THE THREADED BEADS WILL BE UNDERNEATH THE FABRIC.

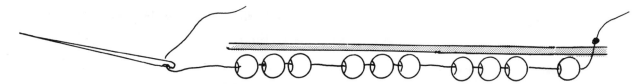

Thread beads under the fabric.

4) With the needle in the left hand, hold the beads taut, push the hook down through the fabric and pull up the thread. A loop will be formed above the frame (wrong side of fabric).

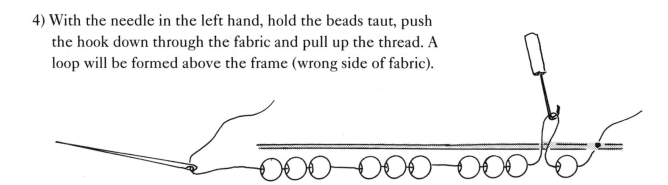

Pull up a loop.

5) Keeping this loop on the hook, slide 2-5 more beads into place, pass the needle down and pull up a second loop through the first one. The first loop should slide off the hook forming a chain stitch.

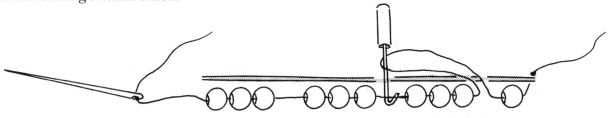

Pull up the second loop.

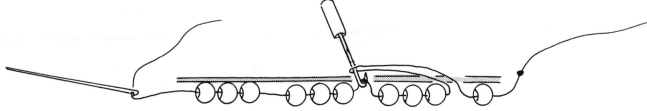

Form a chain stitch.

6) Continue the pattern.

7) Finish off by cutting the thread from the spool leaving about 6". Push the needle up through the fabric, tying a double knot through the last loop and fabric. Clip and glue the knot.

8) On the spool end, clip the thread leaving about 6" of thread. Double knot above the frame. Clip and glue the knot.

COMMON EMBROIDERY STITCHES

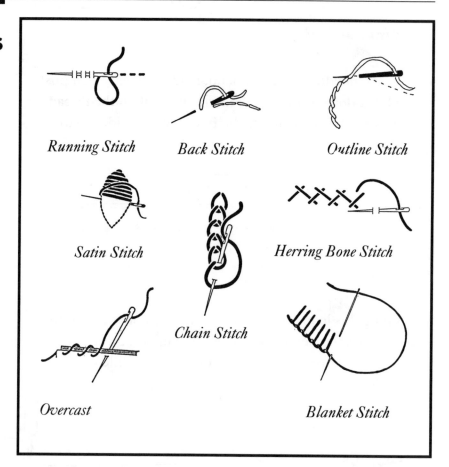

Running Stitch *Back Stitch* *Outline Stitch*

Satin Stitch *Herring Bone Stitch*

Chain Stitch

Overcast *Blanket Stitch*

BEADED NEEDLEPOINT

Part of the beauty of using canvas for bead embroidery is the ready availability and choice of materials and designs. Hand painted and screened canvases, wonderful colors and an endless variety of threads and beads make this decorative art form a relaxing and very creative pastime. Everything from earrings and rings to handbags and decorated "paintings" can be produced with a few basic skills.

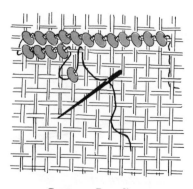

Canvas Beading

72

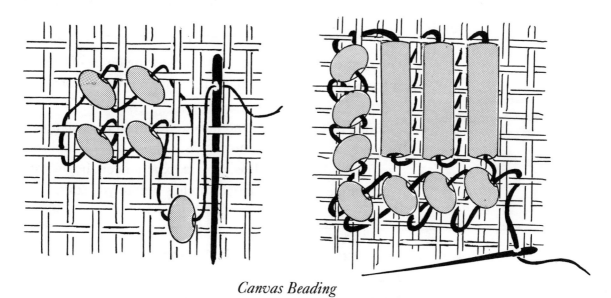

Canvas Beading

Usually made from cotton, polyester or linen threads and coated with sizing for strength, canvas is generally available in widths from 24 to 56 inches. The number of stitches per inch are determined by the number of squares per inch. Eg. size #5 canvas has 5 squares to the inch, size #30 has 30 squares to the inch. Two basic types of canvas are used for needlepoint:

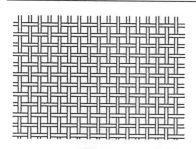

Mono canvas has single threads evenly woven into vertical and horizontal intersecting lines. This forms an open mesh very easy to work.

MONO CANVAS

Mono Canvas

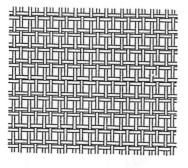

Penelope canvas is double threaded, with 2 vertical closely woven threads and 2 horizontal threads with a small space between them. The four threads are joined at each intersection.

PENELOPE CANVAS

Penelope Canvas

NEEDLES	The needle must be small enough to pass through the canvas and beads. It is a good idea to have an assortment available.
THREAD	Good, strong thread is required for sewing on beads, as lighter threads may tear, particularly if the item is to be worn.
	Needle, thread, canvas and beads should all fit each other properly to insure that the canvas will not be visible through the finished work. Unless you are experienced, begin with a very simple design. Practice stitches before you start.
FRAME	Small canvases can be worked as they are, but an embroidery hoop or wood frame should be used for larger pieces to avoid puckering.

STITCHING THE CANVAS
TO START

Hold a 2" tail of yarn under the canvas with your finger, stitch over it as you work to anchor the yarn.

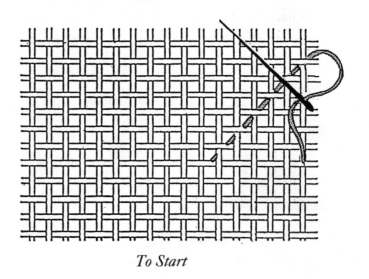

To Start

TO END OFF	ON THE WRONG SIDE, weave a tail of yarn into a few previously worked stitches.

The stitches demonstrated in this section are simple and easy to learn. They represent the most practical variations for this work. They may also be used for beaded needlepoint on perforated wood, plastic or metal backing. All three of these stitches may be referred to as the "Tent" stitch.

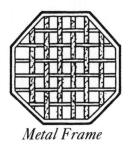

Metal Frame

HORIZONTAL HALF CROSS STITCH

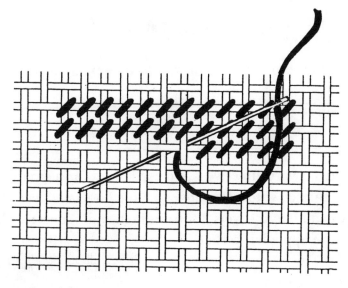

Horizontal Half Cross Stitch

This stitch is worked in horizontal rows across the canvas, starting in the upper left corner.

1) Anchor the yarn

2) Thread a bead, pass the needle down through the mesh of the next square moving to the right.

3) At the end of the row (at the upper right corner), turn the canvas upside down (this keeps the stitches and beads lined up in the same direction)

4) Stitch the next row.

5) Repeat.

VERTICAL HALF CROSS STITCH

This stitch is exactly the same as the horizontal half cross stitch except that the rows are worked up and down, starting in the lower right corner of the canvas.

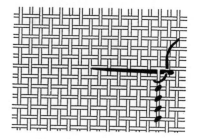

1) Anchor the yarn.

Vertical Half Cross Stitch

2) Thread a bead, pass the needle down through the mesh of the next square directly above.

3) Turn the canvas over or end off at the top of the row.

4) Begin the second vertical row, directly next to the first.

5) Repeat.

UPRIGHT GOBELIN STITCH

This stitch is very effective when used to sew on a group of beads with each stitch. It is done like the horizontal half cross stitch except that it covers 2 squares high and 1 square wide. Start at the upper left corner.

1) Anchor the yarn.

2) Thread on enough beads to cover 2 squares.

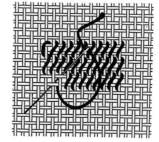

3) Pass the needle straight up 2 squares and into the canvas.

Gobelin Stitch

4) Pass needle down 2 squares (in back) and 1 square to right.

5) Bring up the needle. Thread on beads.

6) Pass the needle up 2 squares and into the canvas.

7) Continue to the end of the row and end off.

8) Begin the next row. Repeat 1-7.

CHAPTER VI

Macrame, Crochet & Knitting with Beads

Macrame with Wood & Bone Beads, Linen Cord

MACRAME, CROCHET & KNITTING WITH BEADS

It's no wonder that among the most popular techniques employed by fiber artists are macrame, crochet and knitting. With just a few basic skills even the novice can create exciting, original work with inexpensive materials. Endless varieties of cord, thread, leather and beads can be utilized for textural richness, intricate shapes and complex designs.

This chapter is meant to serve as a guide for techniques where knowing a little helps you create a lot. If you are a beginner, start with a simple, controlled design, limiting colors and procedure. With carefully selected elements beautiful results can be quickly achieved.

MACRAME

The art of tying knots for utilitarian and aesthetic purpose is called macrame. Incredibly simple and complex at the same time, an amazing array of designs can result from the use of only two basic knots; the half hitch and the square knot.

EQUIPMENT
WORKING SURFACE

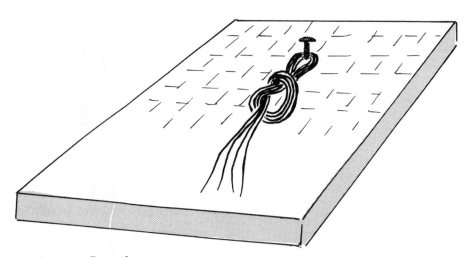

Macrame Board

Some kind of firm surface is needed on which to pin or clip your work. Cork, beaver board, foam rubber, a clip board, or even the back of a chair can be adapted to attach your work. Most craft stores carry an inexpensive board especially designed for macrame work.

Push-pins, hat pins and T-pins will secure your project to the work surface in addition to holding its shape.

You'll need good scissors, a yardstick or tape measure and some rubberbands for bundling cord lengths. Some (colorless) craft glue is good to have on hand to secure the knot ends.

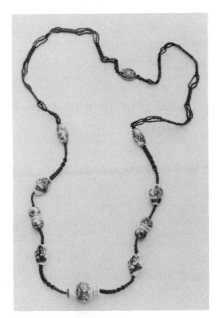

Macrame with Chinese Porcelain Beads

Macrame with Cinnabar Beads and Wood Pendant

Fine linen or cotton cord works well with small, delicate beads; medium heavy cotton or jute is good for larger beads, for both appearance and strength. Nylon is slippery to work and tends to unravel, while wool has a tendency to stretch and break under tension. Leather works extremely well. The choice of beads is infinite, limited only by the design and size of the bore holes.

GENERAL DIRECTIONS

To determine the amount of cord needed, measure about 8 to 10 times the length of the finished piece for each strand.

To prevent tangles (and frustration) with long cords, gather each one up into a "bobbin", about 10" from the project and fasten with a rubberband. Unfasten cord as the work progresses.

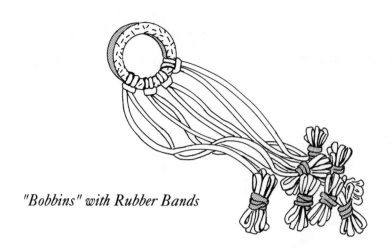

"Bobbins" with Rubber Bands

IF YOU'RE LEFTHANDED, hold a small mirror up to the knot illustrations. The image (and directions) will be reversed.

PRACTICE EACH KNOT you're planning to use until each one has been mastered.

WORK FROM A PLAN sketched on graph paper, with size, color and shaping details, or in free form, creating as you go along.

TO FINISH OFF WITH A FRINGE, thread a bead onto each strand. Tie an overhand knot over and under the bead. Clip and glue the knot.

TO FINISH WITHOUT A FRINGE, cut the cords about 1" long and glue them to the wrong side of the project. Cord ends may also be woven back into the body of the piece, or wrapped as part of the clasp design.

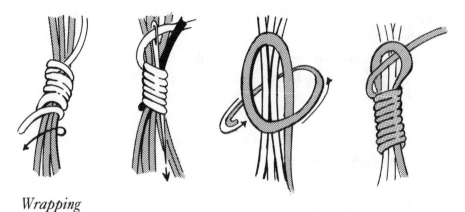

Wrapping

TO SPLICE CORDS, unravel both ends, coat them with white glue, twist them together and allow to dry.

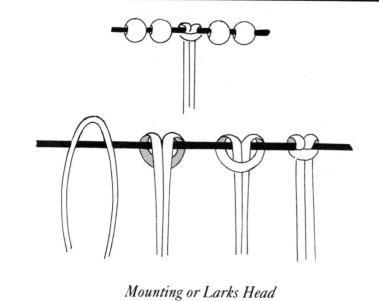

Mounting or Larks Head

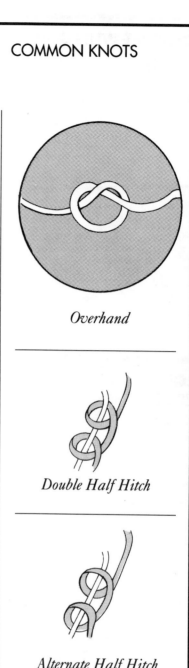

Overhand

Double Half Hitch

Alternate Half Hitch

Reversed Double Half Hitch

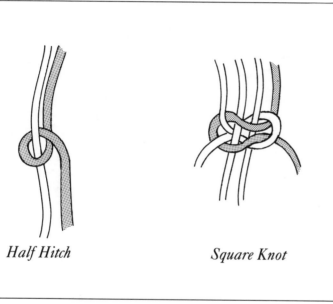

Half Hitch

Square Knot

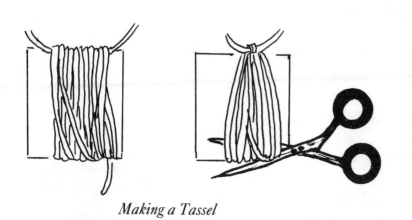

Making a Tassel

CROCHET WITH BEADS

Once the basic stitches are mastered, crocheting with beads can lead to unlimited items. Basically a simple craft to learn, the only supplies needed are the crochet hook, the yarn and the beads.

An infinite range of color and stitches make this a versatile, and stimulating artform. Completely portable, crocheting can express ideas that range from the traditional, to the most avant-garde.

The instructions in this section are purposely simple so that anyone can start with a simple project and advance to more complicated designs. From simple ropes of beads to intricate beaded purses, crochet offers something for everyone.

EQUIPMENT
CROCHET HOOKS

Crochet hooks can be purchased individually or in kits. Available in many stores, the kit is handy to own, as it contains a good selection of hook sizes. For working with beads, a steel or aluminum hook is recommended, as plastic or wood often becomes brittle and can snap under tension.

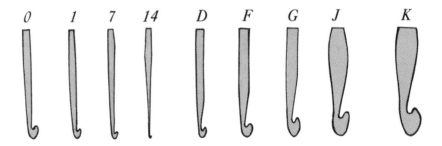

Steel & Aluminum Crochet Hooks

The smallest steel hook is size #14, the largest is 0. In aluminum, the sizes range from B (smallest) to K (largest). The hook you use is generally determined by the thickness of your yarn and desired effect.

YARNS

Almost anything that suits your fancy is suitable for crochet, including FINE WIRE. Whatever you choose,

the bead hole must be large enough to accommodate the cord, and strong enough to support the weight of the beads. (Beginners may find it helpful to seek advice in a good yarn shop or department store).

Tiny complicated patterns require very tiny beads, patience and good eyesight. An experienced and ambitious craftsperson can undoubtedly create a remarkably beautiful item with seed beads, but this section is designed to explain the basic techniques clearly enough to get you started. All types and sizes of beads from glass to plastic, wood and metal are appropriate. The only boundary is design, purpose and level of skill.

BEADS

Have a ruler or tape measure handy, as well as scissors, safety pins and a small box to hold hooks, yarn, needles (for weaving in tail ends), and a basket or bag to hold your work.

MISCELLANEOUS

1) If you are new to crochet, practice and learn the basic stitches before you begin to work with beads. Consider the first few hours an investment in skill. Don't worry about being perfect!

GENERAL DIRECTIONS

2) The Chain Stitch is the foundation for all crochet, as all work is started with a row of chain stitches.

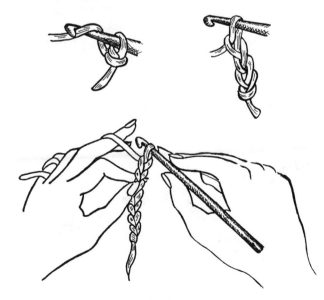

The Chain Stitch

83

3) The Slip Knot, holds the yarn on the hook.

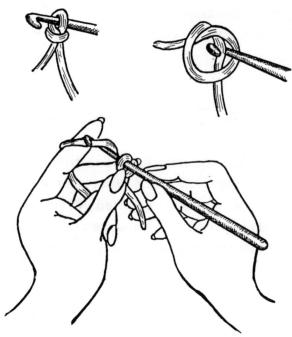

The Slip Knot

4) When all the chains are filled, the work is turned and a new row is begun.

5) Thread on the beads before you begin to crochet. Each bead is passed up individually onto the cord as each stitch is made.

Beads on Spool

6) Work a few rows at a time, starting at the left side of the design.

7) The beads should be kept straight, all slanting in the same direction.

Slant Beads in Same Direction

8) Slip the bead forward onto the cord, secure it with the stitch and then continue.

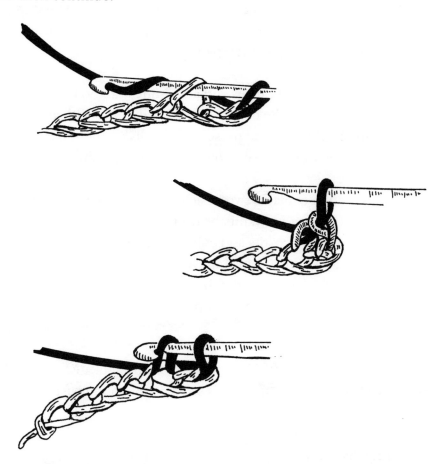

Single & Double Crochet

9) Beautiful, lacy jewelry can be crocheted with beads and lightweight silver or brass wire. Experiment with different gauges and with doubled wire. Elegant pieces are possible with only the chain and single stitch.

KNITTING WITH BEADS

Once the basic principles of knitting have been mastered, you'll find great satisfaction in using your skills to combine yarn or wire with beads. In view of the fact that so many beautiful accessories have survived the ravages of time, one can assume that this rewarding artform attracted numerous craftspeople for a reason.

First of all knitting requires very few, inexpensive basic tools. Second, almost any type of yarn, or fine wire can be used and last, endless patterns, colors and styles can be designed to create unique clothing, purses, belts, jewelry and household articles. Almost any knitted pattern can be beaded.

Elegantly knitted purses and accessories can be found in museums throughout the country. Executed in the 18th and 19th centuries, their careful preservation tells us about our cultural heritage as well as inspire our own knitted "heirlooms."

This section explains two basic methods for knitting with beads. The first way knits beads in at spaced intervales for dramatic borders, accents and color . The second technique, sometimes called "Purse Knitting" adds one or more beads with every stitch. A very solid, fabric-like appearance, results, and the stitches completely disappear.

EQUIPMENT
YARN

Any type of thread can be used for knitting beads, provided the size fits the bore hole, and is strong enough to resist fraying. If this is your first attempt I suggest a soft, slightly stretchy acrylic or nylon upon which to practice. These have the texture of wool, plus strength and washability. As in crochet, make sure you buy enough yarn to complete the whole project.

NEEDLES

Knitting needles range in size from the finest (#00) to the bulkiest (#17) and affect both the gauge and texture of the knitted article. The most important requirement for working with beads is to choose needles that form a loop smaller than the bead; too large a loop permits the bead to slip through to the back of the work.

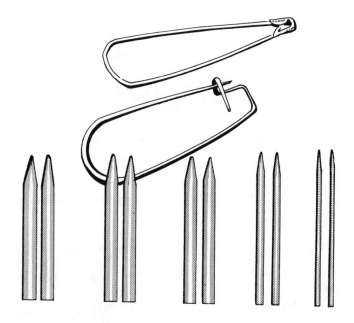

Needles and Stitch Holders

Every design demands its own kind of beads, ranging from lightweight wood, bone, shell or synthetic to heavier gemstones and glass. Since knitting requires a fair amount of time, use good quality beads. If the piece will need laundering or drycleaning, beads should be selected with that in mind. If you are a beginner, start with one size, one color bead and an easy project.

BEADS

You'll need a tape measure to check the gauge, stitch holders to keep work separated, rubberbands or needletips to hold the work when it's put down, and a knitting bag or box for the yarn, needles and beads.

MISCELLANEOUS

CASTING ON

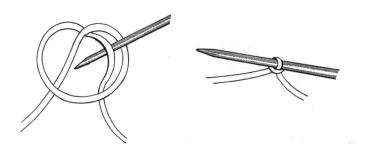

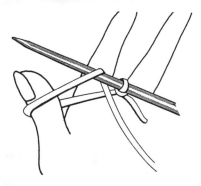

EQUIPMENT

1) "Front" refers to the side of the work facing you, "Back" refers to the side of the work away from you.

2) All knitting starts with loops "cast on" to one needle.

3) Before you begin the pattern, knit a small sample piece to check the gauge. (number of stitches per inch)

4) In bead knitting, all the beads are threaded onto the yarn before you actually begin to knit each row.

5) If a pattern is used, the design should be charted on paper first and followed carefully.

6) All knitting charts are read from right to left.

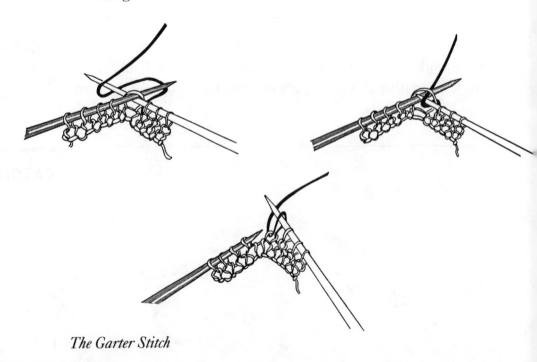

Beads Threaded on Spool

7) Beads must be threaded according to the pattern. The last bead threaded is the first one to be knitted.

8) The "Garter Stitch" refers to a knit stitch in every row, producing a fabric that looks the same on both sides.

The Garter Stitch

9) The "Stockinette Stitch" produces a smooth textured fabric created by alternating rows: one row knit, one row purl.

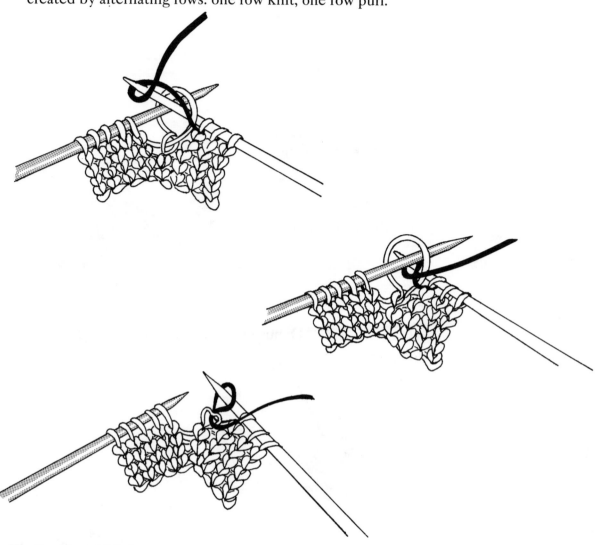

The Stockinette Stitch

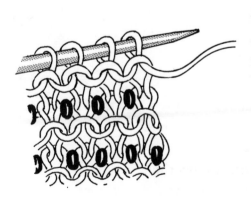

10) To prevent the fabric from curling, beads are generally added in alternate rows: one row plain (no beads), one row with beads.

Add beads in alternate rows.

TO KNIT A BEAD, push it against the back of the needle, take a stitch, then pull the bead through.

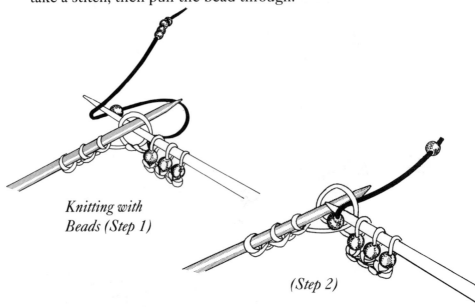

Knitting with Beads (Step 1)

(Step 2)

TO PURL A BEAD, push it against the front of the needle and complete the stitch.

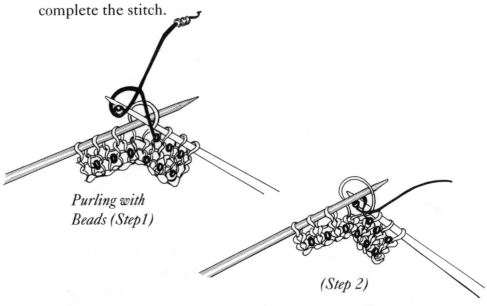

Purling with Beads (Step 1)

(Step 2)

DECREASING, INCREASING, ENDING OFF

TO INCREASE, knit the front of the stitch, and then knit the back of the same stitch, forming two stitches.

TO DECREASE, knit two stitches together.

TO BIND OFF, knit two stitches, then cross the first stitch back over the 2nd one. Continue until the last stitch, then cut the yarn and draw it through the last stitch.

Tube or Spool Knitting

This ancient technique for forming a "chain" is particularly effective with the use of thin wire. (Experiment with 26 to 28 gauge).

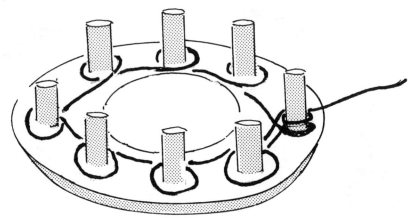

Casting On

1. Cast on one row by passing the cord inside and then around each peg.

2. Second row: Loop the cord around a peg, above the first cord, then lift the lower loop over the one on top, and over the peg.

3. Repeat: one peg at a time. The "chain" will develop downward, inside the central hole.

Lift the lower loop over the one above.

CHAPTER VII

Using Wire and Chain

Inlaid Turquoise, Hematite Beads with Dangles

The secret of smelting metal and combining it with beads was known and applied in Egypt over 5000 years ago. Using superb design, meticulous craftsmanship and durable materials, Egyptian artisans created ornamental pieces with enduring qualities.

Combining beads with wire and/or chain can be very gratifying! Because of its strength, wire can support heavier beads, retain a permanent shape, and serve as a decorative element.

The wonderful part of this chapter is that only a few skills and simple inexpensive tools are required in order to make intricately wired collars, pins, earrings and rings.

EQUIPMENT
FOR BASIC WIRE & CHAINWORK

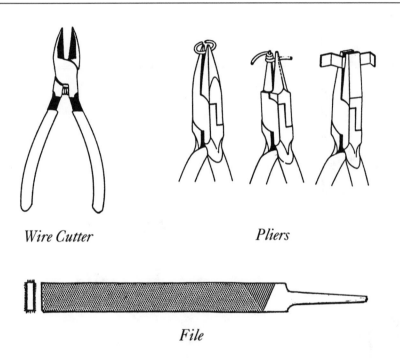

Wire Cutter   *Pliers*

File

Ruler

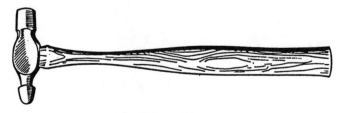

Ball Peen Hammer

OPTIONAL TOOLS

Bench Block

Gauge

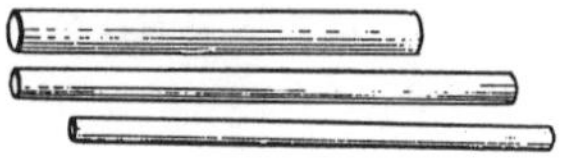

Dowels

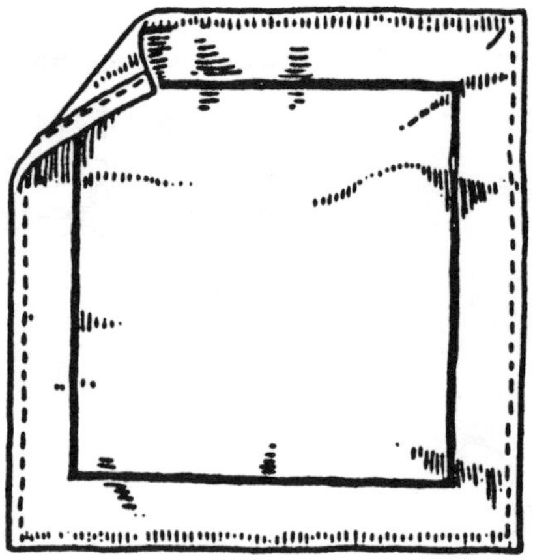

Cloth

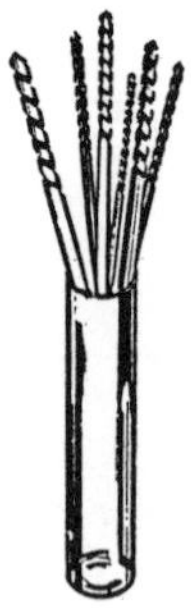

Drill Bits

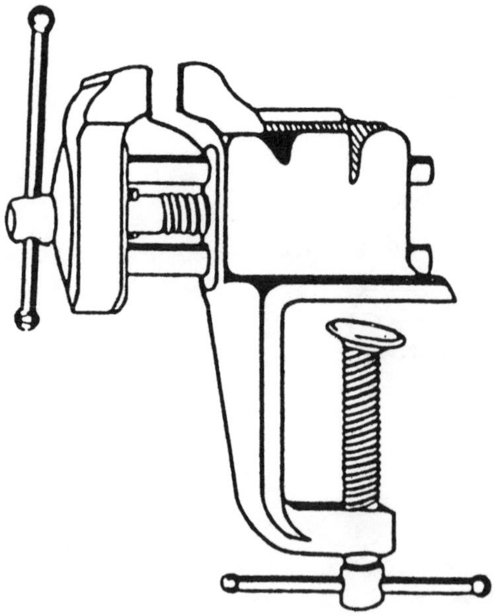

Vise

Hand Drill

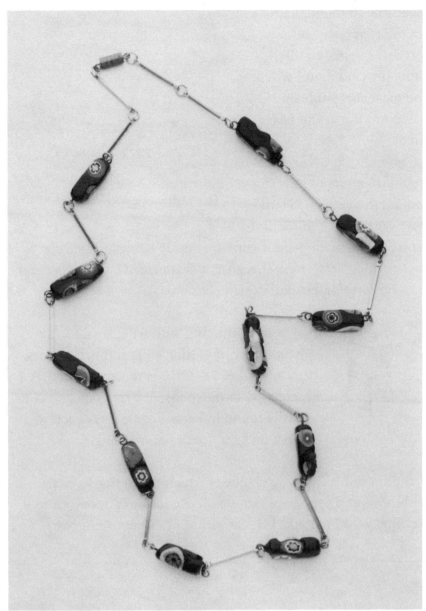

Venetian Beads Strung with Wire

To purchase and use wire, you must be familiar with its gauge, shape and pliability. Gauge describes its size, ranging from very fine thread-like width to slender rods. The lower the gauge, the thicker and heavier the wire.

10	■■■■■■	•	16	——	.	22	——	.
12	■■■■■	•	18	——	.	24	——	.
14	■■■■	•	20	——	.	26	——	.
						28	——	.

Gauge Chart

Available in round, half-round, triangular, tubular, flat and square, you'll probably find round wire the most accessible and easiest to use at the beginning.

Round

Half Round

Square

Triangle

Twist

Wire Shapes

Pliability refers to how soft or hard the wire is. "Hard" wire is extremely difficult to bend, "Half-hard" wire is good for sturdy neck and bracelet pieces, and "soft" wire, (because it is annealed) is flexible, and best for forming beaded design elements.

Spool Wire

If you're stringing with wire, try 22 to 28 gauge. For rings, bracelets and firmer neck-pieces, 14 to 18 gauge is recommended. A selection of inexpensive Brass "spool" wires, easily found in hardware stores is good to have on hand for experimenting.

Last, but not least is the choice of which metal to use. Start with brass and copper. When you feel confident, move on to sterling, goldfilled and 14k, for different effects. (and cost)

BEADS
ANYTHING GOES!

Beaded Collar; Gold Beads with Brass Wire

You may find it expedient to have a few commercial findings on hand before you begin any project. Depending on what you're making, needs will vary. The most commonly used findings are: earring backs (pierced and non-pierced), pin backs, barrette clips, perforated (screen) backs, chain, assorted jump rings and headpins.

Some extremely original and attractive jewelry is made with commercially stamped copper and sterling shapes, combined with wire and beads. These pieces, (with a top hole already drilled) can be purchased from craft stores carrying enameling supplies.

Copper Shapes

GENERAL DIRECTIONS

1) Use a ruler or tape to measure the length of wire you'll need. Cut it cleanly with a wire cutter.

2) Clean the wire before use, using metal cleaner, (or steel wool for brass and copper).

3) File each end of the wire with an even, forward sliding stroke, to remove any rough edges(burrs).

4) For bending, looping and wrapping, use only smooth jawed pliers, as serrated jaws will leave permanent marks on the metal.

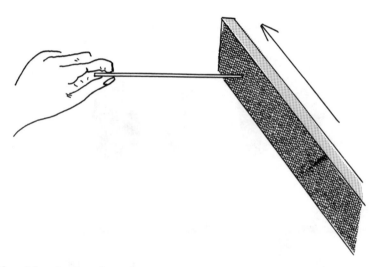

File with a forward stroke.

5) To forge (or form) simple flat shapes, support the metal on a steel bench block (or very hard surface) and hammer until it is flat. File any uneven edges.

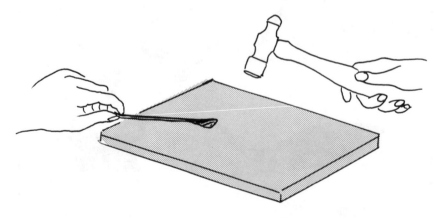

Hammer on a hard surface.

98

6) To bore a hole in metal, use a hand drill or electric drill with small drill bits. Go slowly using light pressure, as drill bits break easily. Always protect your eyes!

Safety Goggles

7) To twist wire for decorative effects, fold the length in half and insert one end (wires together) in a vise or clamp. Insert a pencil or large nail into the folded (loop) end. With the wire taut, slowly turn until the wires are twisted.

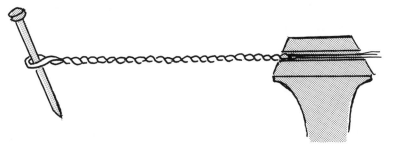

Twisting Wire

8) To straighten wire, lay it on a board, place a small piece of wood on top of the wire, push down hard on the wood and pull the wire. This should straighten "kinks".

9) To bend wire into a sharp angled shape, hold the wire at the edge of the worktable and bend with your pliers.

TO ANNEAL (SOFTEN) METAL

Sometimes, after working it awhile, metal will get hard or brittle and may break. If you are using brass, copper, sterling or 14 karat wire, you can anneal (soften) it without a torch. To anneal with a torch, see Chapter VIII. DO NOT USE THIS TECHNIQUE WITH PLATED OR GOLD-FILLED WIRE!

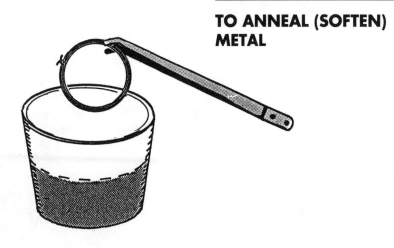

Quench wire in cold water.

1) Fill a pot with cold water and set it to the side of your kitchen stove.

2) Wind the wire into a coil (about 4 inches wide) and grasp the coil with tongs.

3) Light the stove and CAREFULLY move the coil (slowly) back and forth across the heat UNTIL IT TURNS DULL RED. STOP!

4) Quench (drop) the coil immediately into the cold water pot.

5) Dry the wire. If it is discolored, clean it with fine steel wool, metal or silver polish.

HANDCRAFTED FINDINGS

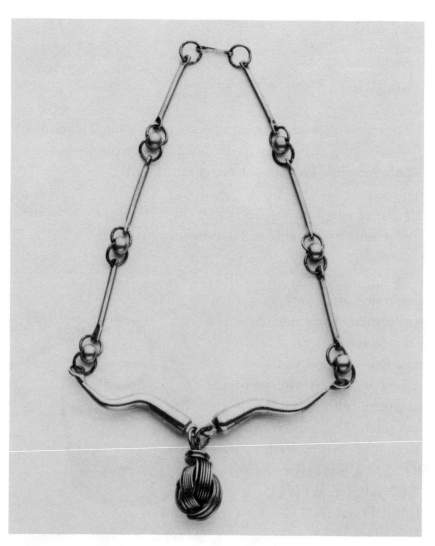

Choker, Silver Wire

Beadwork is an exciting craft all by itself, but combined with handworked wire, it becomes a true art form. The following procedures are for those who wish to put their own creative stamp on their beadwork.

Having an assortment of commercial jump rings on hand is a good idea, but there are often times when it is practical (and fun) to make your own.

TO MAKE TWO JUMP RINGS

1) Use a form for the size and shape you need: eg. a knitting needle, nail, wood dowel, pencil or round nose plier. (if possible clamp the form in a vise)

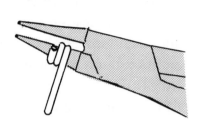

2) Wind the wire tightly around the form until you have two complete circles.

Wind 2 complete circles.

3) Remove the coil from the form.

4) Use your wire cutter to cut through both circles (coils)

5) File the ends smooth

---

1) Wind the wire tightly around the form until you have a multiple coil.

TO MAKE MORE THAN TWO RINGS

2) Cut through the rings one at a time. File each edge. If it is available, use a jeweler's saw to cut through the rings.

Wind a multiple coil.

Wrap the wire around 2 dowels (or nails) held together.

TO MAKE OVAL JUMP RINGS

To make oval jump rings.

WRAPPING

Wrapping is a method of winding wire for decorative or practical purposes. Once you've learned to do this, you'll find endless ways to use this technique. Thick wire can be wrapped to end off a necklace or wound around a single bead or stone and hung on a chain. Two separate elements of a design can be connected with spiral wires, and small wire wound beads can be constructed for unique spacers. This takes some practice, but is well worth the effort.

Wrapping a Stone

1) Use thin gauge soft wire. (22-28 gauge).

2) Cut a piece of wire twice as long as needed.

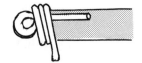

Use wire for Ending

3) Bend one end flat. (about 1/4" to 1/2")

4) Holding the flat end against the "core" (whatever you're wrapping) begin winding the wire tightly (over the flattened section) and around the core.

5) When the wire coil is long enough, clip off the extra wire and tuck the end under the coil.

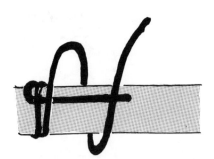

Begin winding the wire.

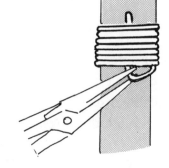

Tuck the end under the coil.

6) Using pliers, gently tighten the coil at both ends.

Crystal Choker, Mirium Haskell (Courtesy of Lil Kleiner)

The device used to open and close or attach beaded elements should always be related to the practical requirements of size, weight and comfort. Nothing is more frustrating than a bracelet which doesn't stay closed, or a necklace that scratches the wearer's neck.

Aesthetically, the fastener should also suit the basic design in scale, color, form and "spirit." The following wire techniques may be considered an avenue to unique and creative design. Although many commercial findings are available, your own handworked elements will stamp your work as original.

EYEPINS

Eyepins are frequently used for earrings, dangles, bead "chains" and bails. Their uses are unlimited.

1) Measure and cut length of wire 1/2" longer than needed. (use 14 to 18 gauge, soft wire)

2) With a round nose plier, grasp the wire about 1/4 inch from the end.

3) Bend the wire into a loop.

4) With plier at the neck of the loop, bend it back to center.

5) Close the loop with the plier.

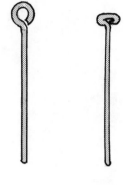

Eyepin   *Headpin*

TO MAKE A WIRE HEADPIN

First make the eyepin. Carefully flatten the loop with a hammer until it closes and forms a metal "knob". Bend this knob back until it forms a pin.

SCROLLS AND S-LINKS

Practice these techniques with 14 to 16 gauge brass or copper wire. Endless design possibilities will emerge for beaded chains, bracelets, earrings and pendants.

1) Cut a few 5" lengths of soft wire. File ends and clean.

Scrolls & S-Links

2) With the tip of a round nose plier, (smooth jaws!) grasp one end of the wire 1/8" from the end.

3) Holding the wire with your other hand, slowly turn the pliers to form a perfect small circle. (This takes practice!) Continue, using fingers and pliers to form a scroll.

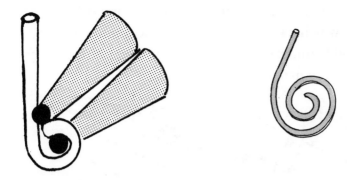

Slowly turn the pliers using the broad part of the pliers.

4) For larger scrolls, keep turning, but reposition the pliers to utilize the broader surface of the plier.

5) After you've made a few scrolls successfully, try making one at the other end of the wire going in the opposite direction in the shape of an "S".

6) With wire cutters and round nose pliers, practice constructing wire forms using varied gauges and sizes.

Form an "S."

7) An alternate way to efficiently curve wire scrolls, is to make a simple "jig" (mechanical assembly device). Using a small board, drive in small nails in the shape desired. Cut off the nail heads. Wrap the wire around the nails using them as a guide. Slide the finished piece off.

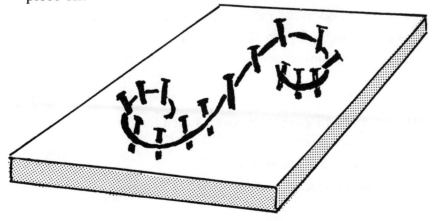

Make a simple "jig."

FORGING OR HAMMERING WIRE

Two tools are needed to forge (hammer) wire: A Ball peen hammer, which has one flat end and one round end, (or a small household hammer), and a smooth flat metal surface (anvil) upon which to hammer.

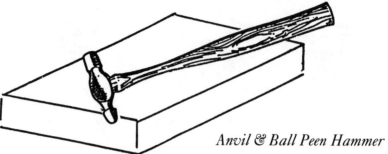

Anvil & Ball Peen Hammer

Changing the shape of wire with a hammer is simple and affords infinite design options. To practice, try the following before you attempt any projects.

1) Choose three or four different gauges of wire, and cut 6" to 8" of each.

2) Lay a wire on the metal surface. Hold one end and strike it with the hammer, progressing evenly from one end to the other.

3) Notice that the wire will curve as you hammer. Turn it over and gently hammer the other side to straighten it.

4) At some point unless it is annealed, the wire will harden (and crack or snap).

Note: Textures from the hammer and metal surface will have been transferred to the metal. This can be an interesting design option, or avoided by wrapping masking tape on the hammer surface. After some experimentation, try the following:

TO MAKE A BEAD "PADDLE"

1) Using 14 to 18 gauge wire cut a 5 inch length.

2) Hold one end of the wire on the metal surface.

3) At one end, hammer one inch flat.

Hammer 1" flat.

4) Test the width by stringing on some beads.

5) If the width is correct, remove the beads and file the paddle edges.

6) String on the beads (or bead)

7) File the un-hammered end.

8) Bend into a "eyepin" for attachment to earrings, necklaces, etc.

NOTE: The paddle can be any length and formed from any metal, and any gauge wire.

String on the beads.

---

1) Form the scroll.

2) Place it on the metal surface.

3) Hammer the scroll evenly along its surface.

TO MAKE HAMMERED SCROLLS

Forged Clasp

1) Cut two 2" lengths of 14 gauge wire.

2) Forge 1/2" of one wire end flat.

TO FORGE A CLASP

3) File off any rough edges.

4) With round nose plier, bend the flattened end to form a hook.

5) Repeat with the second wire.

6) Bend the other ends into jump rings.

NOTE: The clasp may be completely flattened by shaping it into an S, then forging it flat.

*Pearls with Screened Clasp Ends, Mirium Haskell
(Courtesy of Elly Moss)*

Called "caging", this technique is very effective for designing
unusual pins, earrings, rings and clasps. Backing plates are
made in two parts: the "screen", which is a perforated metal
form, and the "plate" which is pronged to hold the screen (plus
pinback, earring back, ring or clasp attachment). Some compa-
nies also make the screens without a backing plate. Both are
available in many shapes and sizes.

When the screen has been completely covered with beads, the
prongs are bent into place, connecting the screen to the back.

You'll need 24 to 28 gauge soft wire, a wire cutter and small
pliers.

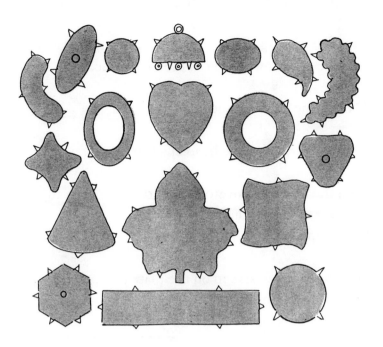

Screens come in many shapes and sizes.

1) Plan your design so that the screen will be completely covered with beads. Begin your first project with a simple design.

2) Hold the screen against the backplate, and mark the four prong positions with a felt marker.

3) Beads can be threaded one at a time, or in whole sections.

GENERAL DIRECTIONS

1) Cut a piece of wire about 12" long

2) Center a bead on the wire

3) Hold the two ends of the wire together and push them through a center hole. The bead should stand upright.

ONE AT A TIME

Threading 1 bead at a time.

109

4) Twist the wire in opposite directions at the back.

5) Bring one wire up through the next hole, thread a bead and push the wire down through the same hole.

6) Do the same with the second wire.

7) Continue wiring on one bead at a time.

8) When the screen is covered, twist the wire ends together, clip off the excess. Use the plier to bend any tails close up into the screen.

9) Place the finished screen on the plate and press the prongs down firmly with pliers.

WHOLE SECTIONS

1) Cut a piece of wire about 12" long.

2) Thread on enough beads to cover the outer rim of the screen.

3) Twist the two ends of the wire together securely, closing the circle of beads.

4) Insert both ends of the wire into the screen, on the outer rim.

5) Holding the beaded circle on the plate, count 3 or 4 holes, thread one wire up through the hole, down over the bead circle and down through the same hole. Pull the wire tight, securing the circle to the plate.

Close circle of beads.

Insert both ends of wire.

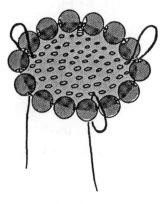

Secure beads to plate.

6) Repeat step 5 going around the circle, until all are fastened.

7) Twist the rest of the wire and clip off excess.

8) Repeat steps 5,6, and 7 until the screen is covered.

9) Attach the screen to the plate.

This section has been added to explore some previously de-scribed wire techniques. It is not meant to be a design manual, but a presentation of simple ideas upon which to build.

BASIC WIRE CHOKER

Wire Choker

This is one of the easiest and most useful wire forms to make. Many variations can be made using this simple procedure. Center a few beads, string the whole wire or add pendants, dangles and/or unique beaded tassels.

To close this choker, use a simple hook & eye closure, avoiding the need for a commercial clasp.

1) Measure the wearer's neck and add 2 inches for the closure.

2) Using 10 to 18 gauge wire, cut wire, clean, and file the ends.

3) With a round nose plier, form a 1/2 inch loop at one end of the wire.

4) Gently bend the wire into a circular form with your fingers, or use a large coffee can or jar to shape the circle.

Form a half inch loop.   *Use a form to shape wire.*

5) Thread on the beads.

6) Measure 3/4 inch beyond the end of the beads. Cut off any excess wire. File the end.

7) With a round nose plier, curve the 3/4 inch of wire into a hook.

8) Shape the choker gently to make sure it forms a circle.

9) For a finished looking clasp, hammer the hooks flat.

WIRE BRACELET

Make a bracelet exactly the same way, except the bracelet should fit the wearer's wrist. (7" is standard size for a bracelet)

DOG COLLAR ON WIRE

"Dog collars" are closely fitting chokers usually containing three or more strands. The beads may be uniform, or an assortment of shapes and colors. Bracelets may be made the same way, omitting a clasp, as soft wire has a spring action allowing it to be easily slipped on and off the wrist.)

1) Lay out your beads. (Each strand will probably be longer than the one above it for proper fit.

2) Measure the wearer's neck, adding 2 inches for the closure.

3) Using 20 gauge wire, cut the wire, clean and file the ends.

4) Using a round nose plier, make a very small loop (about 1/4") at one end of each wire.

5) Thread on the beads, one wire at a time, until all are beaded.

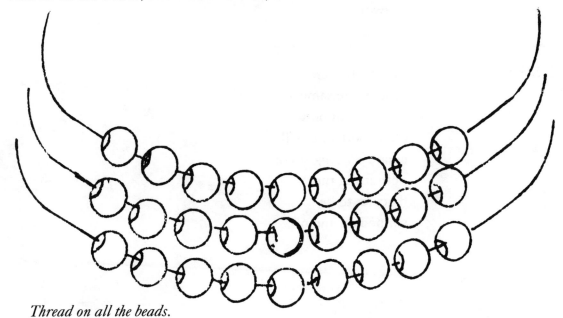

Thread on all the beads.

6) Measure the neckpiece on the neck again, to see if it fits.

7) Measure 1/4 inch beyond the ends of the beads. Cut off excess wire. File the end.

8) Make a 1/4 inch loop at the end of each beaded length.

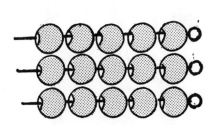

Make a loop at each end.

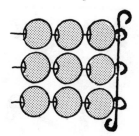

Join strands with wire.

TO JOIN THE STRANDS TOGETHER

1) Using 20 gauge wire, cut two 3 inch lengths. Clean and file.

2) With a round nose plier, make a loop at the top of the joined strands.

113

3) Clip off the excess wire, then make another loop at the
   bottom of the joined strands.

4) Attach a commercial hook and eye clasp to the loops (or
   make one with 20 gauge wire and your round nose plier!) If
   your beads are heavy, use 12-14 gauge wire for the hook and
   eye)

MULTIPLE STRAND BRACELET

Make a bracelet
exactly the same
way, except omit the
clasp. Soft wire will
create a spring action
permitting the
bracelet to be
slipped on and off.

EARRINGS
DANGLES

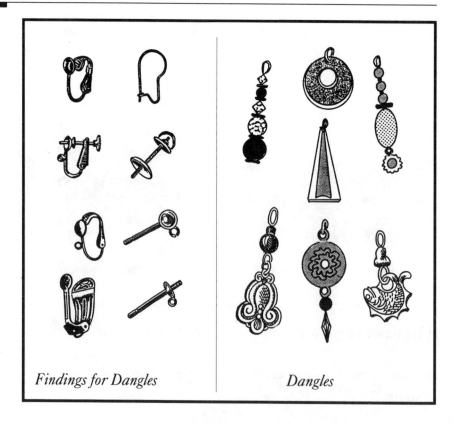

Findings for Dangles   *Dangles*

1) Use commercial earring findings of all types to attach dangles.

2) Try a flat pad earring back upon which to glue a button or flat backed stone. Epoxy a wire jump ring to the back of the button, and attach beads, tassels or wire shapes.

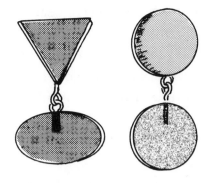

Button or Stone Dangles

---

1) Use two flat earring backs. Attach a flat button or metal shape with epoxy.

Attach button to earring back.

BEADED "BUTTONS"

2) Using soft light wire, string approximately 6 inches of beads. Make a tiny loop at one end.

3) Going in a circle around the button, test to see if the beaded circle will cover the form. Adjust number of beads.

4) Clip the excess wire, leaving about 1/4 inch at each end.

5) Make a tiny loop at the end of the wire so the beads are secure at both ends.

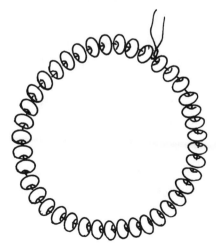

Secure the beads.

115

6) Attach the circle of beads to the form with epoxy.

7) Try making two or three layers of beads in different shapes. Experiment with different shapes and sizes. Glue on a jump ring attachment and add dangles.

8) Using (commercial) flat bezel forms, button earrings can be constructed with bead nuggets (chips) epoxied inside the bezel, and then connected to an earring (or ring) backing. Dangles can be attached.

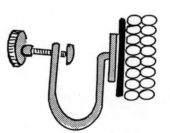
Two layers of beads.

Use bezel and chips.

PINS AND BARRETTES

There are a few ways to construct beaded pins and a variety of commercial pin and barrette backs from which to choose.

Pin, Mirium Haskell

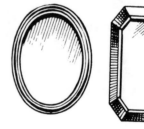
Commercial Bezels

1) Use a flat metal (or bezel) form upon which to epoxy a beaded design. Epoxy the form to a pin back.

2 Use an antique or interesting belt buckle, epoxied to pin back. Add dangles.

3) Epoxy a jump ring (or rings) to the back of a costume or stone pin and add bead dangles.

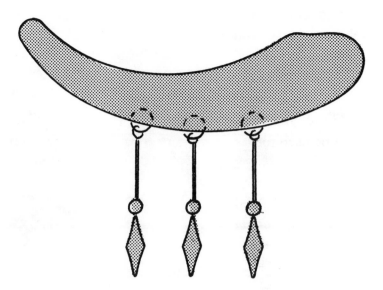

Attach pin back and dangles.

4) Using 10 to 14 gauge wire, make a simple shape: circle, square, triangle, rectangle.

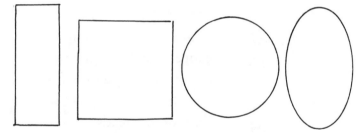

Make simple wire shapes.

Using 16 to 18 gauge wire, lay out bead rows to fit vertically or horizontally across the wire "frame". Attach the beaded rows by looping the wire around the edges of the frame.

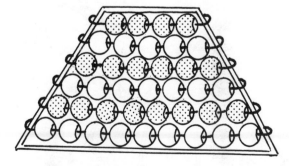

Loop the wire around the frame.

With 16 to 18 gauge wire, attach the pin back to the beading wire, by "sewing" it on. Clip off excess wire. (Be sure there are no tails to tear clothing).

Add fringes, dangles, tassels or whatever your imagination brings to mind.

NOTE: These same techniques can be used for barrettes.

Silver Beads & Wire "Cluster" Earrings

RINGS

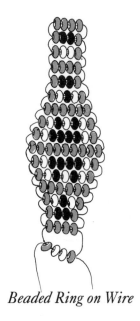

Beaded Ring on Wire

1) Use about 2 feet of 28 gauge wire and crossneedle techniques for many interesting rings. (also bracelets and chokers!)

2) Thread one, two or three beads on to the middle of about 4" of 12 to 14 gauge wire. Cross the wire through the beads in opposite directions. Test for size. Wrap the wire at both sides of the beads.

3) Use a commercial ring setting with beaded screen epoxied on.

Combining Handmade Findings with Precut Shapes

CHAPTER VIII

Drilling, Sawing & Soldering

Silver Beads with Soldered Tubes on Leather

This chapter is meant to be exciting, to inspire all kinds of new ideas and to present the basic skills of metalsmithing. If you've never picked up a drill, or sawed, or soldered before, you'll find these techniques surprisingly uncomplicated, enjoyable and satisfying.

Using any one of the methods described, your beadwork can move onto a brand new level of design, and inventiveness. Wonderful possibilities for enhancing your work come from being able to drill, or solder components, to shape unique metal pieces, and to convert antique buckles or pins to pendants. These skills can deepen your involvement with beaded jewelry in many ways.

SAFETY RULES

THESE SAFETY RULES SHOULD BE FOLLOWED CAREFULLY:

1) ALWAYS PROTECT YOUR EYES WITH SAFETY GOGGLES WHEN DRILLING OR SAWING.

2) USE A BRUSH (NOT YOUR HANDS) TO SWEEP ALL WORK SURFACES, AS FILINGS AND METAL SHAVINGS CAN BE SHARP.

3) IF YOU DO ANY SOLDERING, KEEP A SMALL FIRE EXTINGUISHER IN A CONSPICUOUS PLACE.

4) IF YOU ARE USING ANY ELECTRIC POWER TOOL, WEAR RUBBER SOLED SHOES. MAKE SURE THE TOOL IS GROUNDED AND UNLESS YOU ARE FULLY TRAINED NEVER OPERATE THE TOOL NEAR OR WITH WATER.

5) HAVE A SECURE LOCKING PROCEDURE TO KEEP SMALL CHILDREN OR PETS SAFELY FROM YOUR TOOLS.

Since these directions are intended for inexperienced met-alsmiths, it would be wise to use only copper and brass until you're confident about your skills. For skills beyond the basic procedures covered here, there are many excellent jewelry making books, as well as community colleges and adult education classes, where more detailed instruction is available.

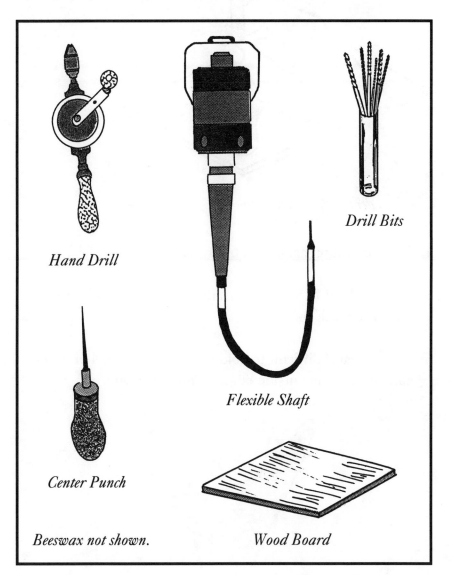

Hand Drill

Drill Bits

Flexible Shaft

Center Punch

Beeswax not shown.

Wood Board

1) Place your work on the wooden board.

2) Insert the drill bit into the chuck of the drill, with about 1/4" protruding.

3) With a nail (or center punch) and hammer, make a dent in the metal exactly where you want the hole.

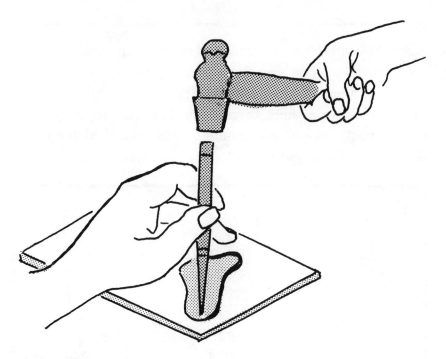

Make a dent with the center punch.

4) Rub the drill bit across the beeswax.

5) Holding the drill upright, turn the handle and drill through until you reach the board.

6) If the metal is difficult to hold in place, hammer 4 or 5 small nails around the outside edges to hold it steady.

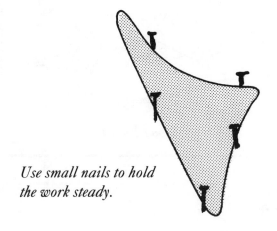

Use small nails to hold the work steady.

7) File away any rough edges.

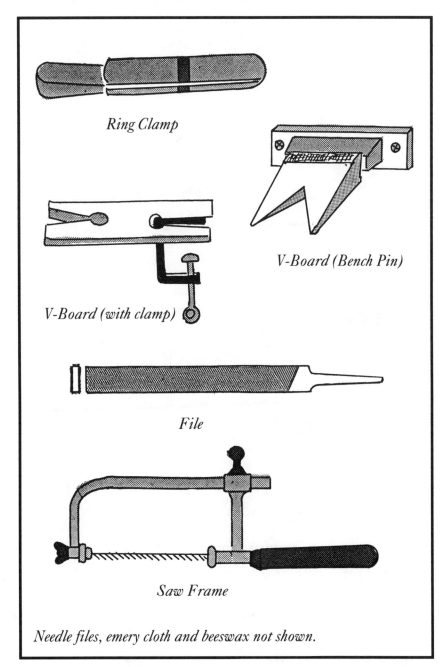

Ring Clamp

V-Board (Bench Pin)

V-Board (with clamp)

File

Saw Frame

Needle files, emery cloth and beeswax not shown.

Sometimes the hardest part of sawing is inserting the saw blade properly. Because they are fragile, they easily snap under tension (even when you're inserting them!)

INSERTING THE BLADE

1) Loosen the wing screws at each end of the frame.

2) With the teeth pointing DOWN and OUT from the frame, insert the blade into the top of the frame and tighten the screw.

3) Press the top of the frame against the edge of the work table, holding it slightly compressed.

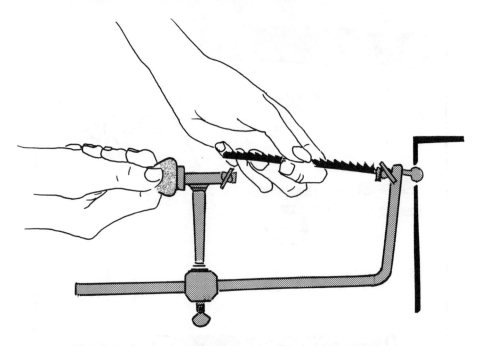

Press the frame against the work table to insert the blade.

4) Insert the other end of the blade in the lower clamp and tighten the screw. Release the pressure.

5) The blade should be taut and straight and make a pinging sound when plucked.

SAWING

1) Wax the blade with beeswax.

2) Place the metal on the benchpin.

3) Hold the saw frame in a vertical position and begin the cut with two or three gentle upward strokes.

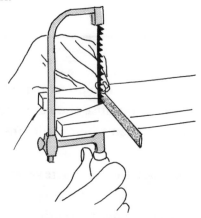

4) Saw with the whole length of the blade in downward stroke, cutting as the blade moves down and releasing pressure as it moves up.

Saw with straight downward stroke.

5) To turn a corner, move the blade up and down in very short strokes while you slowly turn the metal with the other hand.

6) To remove the blade, GENTLY back it out of the cut, (or release one end of the blade and pull it through.)

To remove a center (or hole) section of metal:

PIERCING

1) Using an anvil as support, make a dent with a center punch or nail within the area that will be removed.

2) Drill a hole large enough for the saw blade to fit.

3) Release one end of the saw blade and insert it through the hole. Retighten the blade. Cut out the metal.

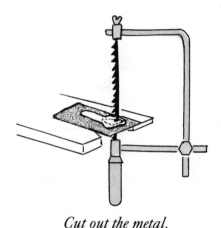

4) When the whole section has been cut, loosen one screw, remove the blade and the cut-out piece.

Cut out the metal.

Sharp edges will probably remain after any drilling and/or sawing, and must be filed smooth.

FILING

1) Use as large a file as the work will permit.

2) Hold the work in your hand, a ring clamp or vise, and brace it against the work table edge.

3) Using the whole length of the cutting edge, apply pressure on the FORWARD stroke.

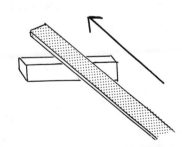

4) Remove any remaining scratches with medium emery cloth or paper, sanding in one direction.

File on the forward stroke.

125

Antique Silver Pins. Soft Soldered Rings Hold Beads.
Pin Back Filed Off (Left)

Permanently connecting two pieces of metal together, using a melted, softer metal to join them, is called soldering.

GENERAL DIRECTIONS

Whichever methods or metals you use, the following rules always apply:

1) The metal must be clean. Use metal cleaner, steel wool, or a mixture of ammonia and water to remove any surface film.

2) Choose the correct solder and flux by checking the manufacturer's instructions. Make sure that all surfaces to be soldered are covered with flux.

3) The surfaces to be joined must fit together perfectly. (Solder does not fill gaps)

4) The right amount of solder must be placed in the right places.

5) The metal must be heated just enough to melt the solder and cause it to flow.

6) Solder always flows toward the source of heat.

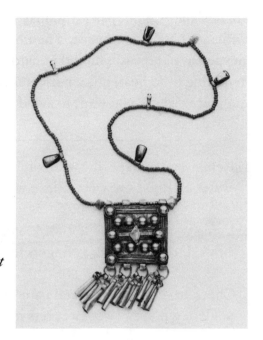

Ethiopian Silver Pendant Soldered and Worked with Wire and Beads

SOLDERING WITH A SOLDERING IRON
EQUIPMENT

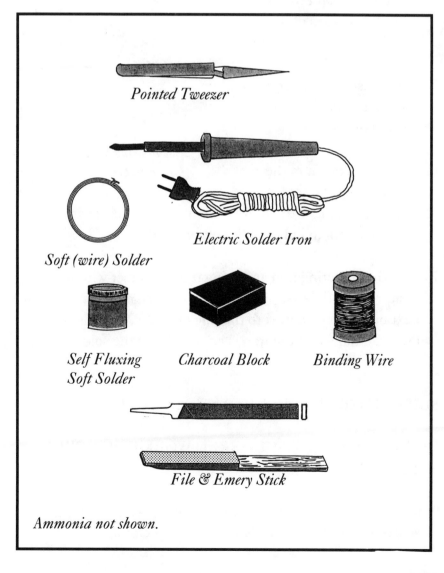

Pointed Tweezer

Electric Solder Iron

Soft (wire) Solder

Self Fluxing Soft Solder

Charcoal Block

Binding Wire

File & Emery Stick

Ammonia not shown.

For designing and repairs, you may find this technique is sufficient for all your needs. The iron, solder and flux are inexpensive and easily found in hardware and craft stores. Requiring little heat, it is a perfect technique for simple repairs and pieces where you want to avoid glue.

GENERAL DIRECTIONS

1) Remove all surface dirt with kitchen cleanser, ammonia and water, or fine steel wool. Rinse well in running water.

2) Using tweezers, place the work on a charcoal block or fire-brick. Do not handle, as fingers leave dirt.

3) Check to see that the metal parts are in perfect contact at the soldering points. (Use tweezers to rearrange)

4) Completely paint or cover both facing sides of the metal with soft solder flux.

5) With scissors or cutter, snip solder into tiny pieces.(snippets)

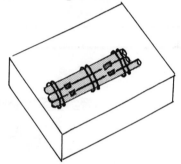

Use binding wire for perfect contact.

6) Dip a small brush in the flux, pick up the solder snippets and place them in position. (Experiment with scrap pieces to learn to judge solder placement).

7) Heat the soldering iron and bring it into contact with the metal. When the first piece of solder melts, move on to the next piece, staying next to the line of solder, but not on it. (You can tell when the iron is hot enough if the solder melts instantly when touched).

8) After all solder is melted, let the metal air cool.

DO NOT PUT SOFT SOLDERED WORK IN A PICKLE SOLUTION.

9) Remove excess solder by filing or sanding, or by melting the solder and wiping away the excess with a cloth.

Antique Coin Soldered for Stringing

The greatest advantage of torch soldering is it versatility. After you've soldered a few practice pieces you may find this to be the most important technique so far!

Essentially the same as soft (iron) soldering, this procedure uses a flame as the source of heat, and must be "pickled" between solderings to remove fire scale. Since medium and hard solders can be used, and the solder actually penetrates the metals being joined, a much stronger and more permanent bond is possible. In addition, one piece can be constructed with a number of soldered joints, using hard, medium and soft solder, in that order.

The torch offers enormous design freedom. You'll find it indispensable for annealing, for soldering jump rings, bails, earrings, pinbacks and for making your own clasps and pendants. Do lots of practicing on brass and inexpensive jewelry before you tackle precious metals. For more advanced techniques, consult metal-smithing books and classes.

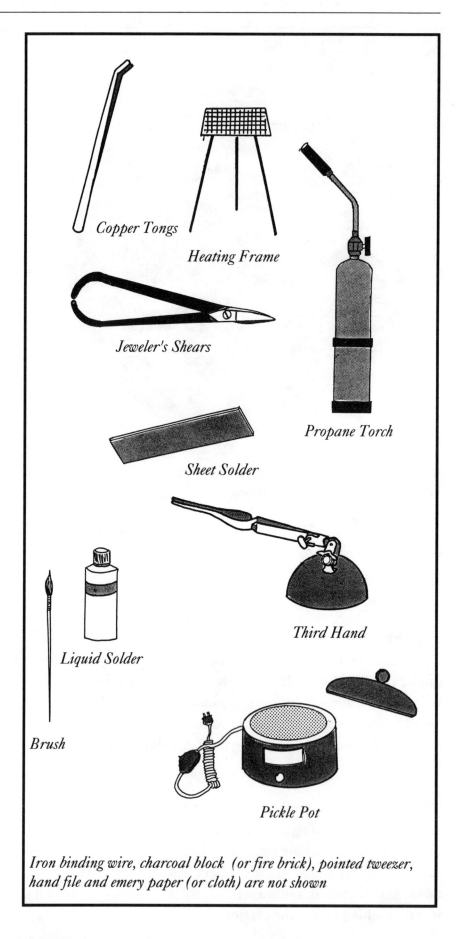

Copper Tongs

Heating Frame

Jeweler's Shears

Propane Torch

Sheet Solder

Third Hand

Liquid Solder

Brush

Pickle Pot

Iron binding wire, charcoal block (or fire brick), pointed tweezer, hand file and emery paper (or cloth) are not shown

ALWAYS FOLLOW THE MANUFACTURER'S DIRECTIONS FOR TORCH USE. NEVER LEAVE THE FLAME UNATTENDED, OR WHERE IT COULD ENDANGER ANYTHING AROUND IT. ALWAYS POINT THE TIP AWAY FROM YOU, AND NEVER PUT YOUR FINGERS OR FACE NEAR THE FLAME. BECAUSE OF THEIR TOXIC QUALITIES AVOID THE USE OF ANY ASBESTOS EQUIPMENT AND ANY FLUX WHICH IS FLUORON BASED.

GENERAL DIRECTIONS

1) Make certain that all the surfaces to be soldered are perfectly fitted. (Use iron binding wire or brads to hold the pieces together)

2) Remove gemstones.

3) Clean the work thoroughly.

4) Apply flux on the areas to be soldered.

5) Lay a tiny solder "snippet" at each of the joints.

6) Adjust the flame to medium, (a medium bluish flame) and move the heat around the joint area (not on the solder) until the solder flows. Solder should flow within 6 to 10 seconds!

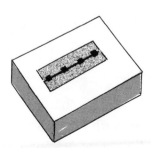 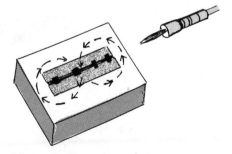

Lay snippets along the joint.   *Move the flame around the joint areas.*

7) Using copper tongs, place the work in the pickle ("Sparex") solution for a few minutes.

8) Remove the work with copper tongs and rinse in clean water.

9) Turn off the torch.

10) File and polish the work.

FLAME ADJUSTMENTS

Flame adjustments needed for various applications:

REDUCING: This is a very soft "bushy" yellow flame with a small dark blue cone inside. Use only for annealing.

NEUTRAL OR MEDIUM: (also called "normal" flame). This has a gentle hissing sound, and a medium bluish color. This is the flame to use for all normal soldering.

OXIDIZING: This flame has a very strong hissing sound, a light blue cone and small dark blue point. It is a "hard" flame and should be avoided.

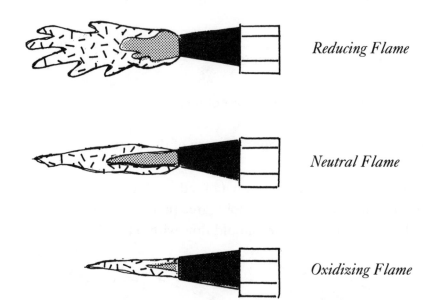

Reducing Flame

Neutral Flame

Oxidizing Flame

SOLDER

Solder comes in sheet, wire and stick form, and in hard, medium and soft melting temperatures. Start with extra easy or easy solder, and use only enough to make a smooth joint. (This takes practice). To prepare solder for use, cut tiny snippets from the sheet or wire. (Keep all solders in labeled containers, separated by hardness and metal content).

Cut tiny snippets of solder.

Flux prevents the formation of oxides (fire scale) and helps solder flow. Available in solid, powder, paste and liquid forms, a borax based flux is best for general use. "Handy" flux, (a paste) is good for beginners.

FLUX

Once metal has been heated it must be cleaned. This is done by immersing the piece in "pickling" solution and then rinsing it thoroughly in water. Many professionals use a toxic mixture containing sulphuric acid, but because it is much safer, use "Sparex", a non-corrosive powder that dissolves in water.

PICKLING

Pickle is most effective when hot and must be stored in a covered glass or stoneware pot. (A small electric crockpot works perfectly!). After pickling and rinsing in water, the piece should be neutralized to remove any remaining acid. Soak the piece for about five minutes in a warm solution of baking soda (sodium bicarbonate) and water, (2-3 TB of soda in a cup of water).

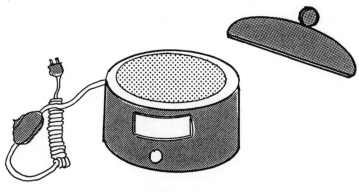

Pickling Pot

Metal becomes hard and brittle when continuously twisted, pounded or bent, and must be annealed. Coat the piece with flux, flame heat it to a deep red color, and quench it in water. Pickle to remove fire scale and flux.

ANNEALING

133

POLISHING

After working the metal, sandfinish your piece with emery or carborundum paper, progressing from medium to fine grits.

Hand buffing to a high polish can be accomplished using Tripoli and Rouge on a piece of chamois or leather, glued to a flat stick. Use Tripoli first to remove fine scratches and then Rouge for the final polish. Keep each compound and buffing stick separated.

Motorized polishing is easily done if you have a flexible shaft tool. Use polishing wheels of felt, cloth or chamois charged (or rubbed) with each buffing compound.

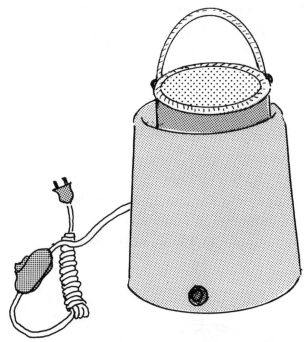

An ultrasonic cleaner will keep your jewelry bright and shiny.

APPENDICES

Beads, Metals & Adhesives

BEADS
Standard Terminology, Measurements and Shapes, Number of Beads Needed, Care and Cleaning, Needles and Threads, Stone Testing

METALS
Quality Marks, Melting Temperatures, Antiqueing, Standard Weights and Measures

ADHESIVES
Types of Glues, Application and Solvents

BEADS
STANDARD TERMINOLOGY

Beaded jewelry is generally described by standard terms and lengths. These measurements always include the clasp.

BIB
A necklace with three or more strands, with each one longer than the one above it.

BRACELET
A 7" length for the wrist.

CHOKER
Usually 16". A uniform necklace that drops to just above the collarbone.

DOG COLLAR
A necklace of three or more strands worn close on the neck.

GRADUATED
A necklace of gradually increasing size beads, with the smallest near the clasp, and the largest at the center.

LARIAT
A necklace of 48" (or longer) that is not joined at the ends, but tied in a knot or wrapped around the neck.

MATINEE
A necklace 20" - 24" in length.

OPERA
A necklace 28" - 32" in length.

PRINCESS
A necklace 18" in length.

ROPE
A necklace 40" - 45" or longer

UNIFORM
A necklace of any length, with equal sized beads throughout.

Beads are available in three forms:

Ball
(Undrilled)

Bead
(Drilled Through)

1/2 Drilled
(For Pegsetting)

Beads come in all shapes, materials and sizes, but they are almost always measured by millimeters (1/25 of an inch). Gemstone beads and pearls are sold in temporarily strung 16" lengths. The following measurements are helpful in determining necessary supplies. (Some beads vary slightly)

16" TEMPORARILY STRUNG			
SIZE	BEADS	SIZE	BEADS
3mm	128	10mm	40
4mm	100	11mm	36
5mm	80	12mm	33
6mm	66	14mm	29
7mm	57	16mm	25
8mm	50	18mm	23
9mm	45	20mm	20

Calibrated Bead Sizes

20mm   *18mm*   *16mm*   *14mm*   *12mm*   *10mm*   *9mm*   *8mm*   *7mm*   *6mm*   *5mm*

SEED BEADS are sold loose in small packages, by the string (20") and by the Hank (usually 12 strings per hank).

APPROXIMATE NUMBER OF BEADS PER INCH					
Size	1"	20"	Size	1"	20"
#16	28	560	#11	18	340
#14	25	465	#10	16	295
#13	24	415	#9	12	240
#12	21	370			

DETERMINING NUMBER OF BEADS NEEDED

Use the chart or the following formula:

1" = 25.4mm

If your necklace is to be 15" long using 6mm beads:

1. Multiply 25.4(mm) by 15 (inches)
   25.4 x 15 = 381(mm)
2. Divide 381(mm) by 6 (mm/bead)
   381/6=63.5(beads)

The result: 63.5 is the number of 6mm beads needed for a 15" necklace.

mm	1"	7"	16"	24"	32"	36"

APPROXIMATE NUMBER OF BEADS PER INCH						
mm	1"	7"	16"	24"	32"	36"
3	8.25	57	132	200	265	288
4	6.25	43	100	150	200	225
5	5.00	35	82	124	160	180
6	4.25	28	67	100	132	153
7	3.50	24	57	85	114	126
8	3.25	22	50	75	100	112
9	2.75	19	45	67	90	101
10	2.50	18	40	60	80	90
12	2.00	15	33	50	66	72
14	1.75	13	29	43	56	63
16	1.50	11	25	38	50	54
18	1.25	10	23	34	45	50
20	1.20	8	20	29	38	43

Since some beads may be of poor quality (poorly drilled, cracked or discolored), it is wise to have a few extra beads on hand. Subtract the width of spacers and clasp before stringing.

COMMON & SPECIAL BEAD SHAPES

1 - Globular
2 - Barrel
3 - Pear
4 - Cylinder
5 - Tubular
6 - Lozenge
7 - Oblate
8 - Oval (Elipsoid)
9 - Cube
10 - Collared
11 - Tabular
12 - Annular
13 - Melon
14 - Capped
15 - Faceted
16 - Lenticular
17 - Rectangular
18 - Hexagonal
19 - Trigonal
20 - Verticle Spacer
21 - Segmented
22 - Convex Bicone
23 - Concave Bicone
24 - Horizontal Spacer

Based on Beck's Terminology & Vander Sleen's Drawings

All beads can be immersed in warm, soapy water for a few minutes, gently scrubbed with a soft brush, rinsed and laid flat to dry on a soft towel.

Glass, metal and most stone beads can benefit from an ultrasonic bath, with the exception of the following, which might be permanently damaged: Amber, Bone, Coral, Horn, Ivory, Opal, Pearls, Plastic, and Turquoise.

SHELLS found on the beach may be soaked in a solution of Clorax and water for a day or two, then thoroughly rinsed. If you decide to drill, (wear safety glasses!) drill slowly. Start with a small size bit and enlarge the hole with gradually larger bits.

QUILLS are sharp, and should be handled with care. To clean, they may be soaked in detergent and water for a few hours, or placed in boiling water for a few minutes, then rinsed and laid flat to dry.

To trim quills to size (wear safety glasses!) use a nail clipper or wire cutter, then clean the spongy interior with a long, sharp needle.

The higher the number, the smaller the needle. Basically, you use a size #10 (or higher) needle with size 10 beads.

I. LONG NEEDLE: Made in England. Used for loom work. Size #10 is the largest and Size #16 the smallest.

II. SHARPS NEEDLE: Made in England. Used for beading fabric or thin leather, peyote, and lazy stitch.

III. TWISTED NEEDLE: A long, finely twisted wire with a collapsible eye. Generally classified as Fine (#6)/Med (#10)/Heavy (#12),these are for stringing pearls and beads.

IV. GLOVER'S NEEDLE: Has a three-sided sharp point and large eye to accommodate heavy thread. Especially made for working with leather. Size #1 is the largest, Size #9 the smallest.

THREADS

Always try to use the heaviest thread that will pass through the bore holes, and support the weight of the beads. In carded cords, #0 is the thinnest, #16 the heaviest. Spool threads generally start with #000 and progress by letters to #FFF

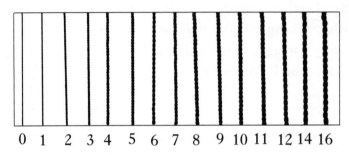

0 1 2 3 4 5 6 7 8 9 10 11 12 14 16

Silk or Nylon Card Sizes

Spool Threads: Size E (doubled)=Size 4
                        Size FF(doubled)=Size 8
                        Size FFF(doubled)=Size 16

SIMPLE STONE TESTING

Stone beads are not always what they appear to be. To determine whether they are genuine, dyed, or glass imitations, use the following simple techniques.

ACETONE TEST: Use a cotton swab or soft cloth, and moisten it with acetone (nail polish remover). Rub the cotton over one of the stones. If the cotton becomes discolored, the stone has been dyed.

USING A LOUPE: Examine the bore hole and any surface blemishes. If the beads are dyed, you'll often see a line between the natural and dyed color of the stone, and dark concentrations of color in surface cracks.

USING A FILTER: Use a polarizing filter, (or a pair of Poloroid sunglasses). Hold the stone up to the light and rotate it 180 degrees. Most colored stones will show some change in shade or color, but glass shows NO color change. When in doubt, use a loup to look for bubbles and swirl marks, and examine the facet edges very carefully; they are usually not as sharp, or distinct as in genuine stones.

GOLD:"Karat" describes the amount of gold in an alloy. An alloy containing less than 10 Karats may not be legally classified as precious metal.

24K	= 1.000	= Pure Gold
22K	= .917	= 91.7% Pure Gold
18K	= .750	= 75.0% Pure Gold
16K	= .667	= 66.7% Pure Gold
14K	= .585	= 58.5% Pure Gold
12K	= .500	= 50.0% Pure Gold
10K	= .417	= 41.7% Pure Gold

SILVER:

Fine Silver	= .999	= Pure Silver
Sterling Silver	= .925	= 92.5% Silver
Coin Silver	= .900	= 90% Silver/10% copper

Nickel or German Silver = Has no silver: an alloy of 65% copper, 18% zinc, 17% nickel.

GOLD FILLED: Layers of gold are welded to a base metal, and must weigh 1/20 or more of the total weight.

12K/20 GF: 1/20 is 12K Gold

14K/20 GF: 1/20 is 14K Gold

VERMEIL: 120 Micro inches of 10K (or more) gold is bonded to Sterling Silver Base Metal.

BRASS	= 75% copper and 25% zinc
BRONZE	= 90% copper and 10% tin
PEWTER	= 92% tin and 8% antimony

MELTING POINTS OF METALS (FARENHEIT)

Tin	= 450°	Silver (Fine)	= 1760°
Pewter	= 450° - 500°	Gold 24K	= 1945°
Brass	= 920° -930°	Gold 14K	= 1475°
Aluminum	= 1220°	Bronze	= 1945°
Silver (Coin)	= 1615°	Copper	= 1981°
Silver (Sterling)	= 1640°	Platinum	= 3220°

TO ANTIQUE (OXIDIZE)

Using a toothbrush dipped in ammonia and water, thoroughly clean the metal. Rinse well. Following label directions, heat a solution of "Liver of Sulfer" (potassium sulfide). DO NOT BOIL! With tweezers, dip the piece into the solution (check its progress), or apply the solution with a brush to the desired areas. Allow to dry, then buff off the areas where you don't want oxidation. Household bleach (Clorox) may also be used (with care!) on silver. When the desired shade is reached, wash the item with water.

STANDARD WEIGHTS AND MEASURES

TROY WEIGHT: Used in weighing precious metals.
1 Troy oz = 31.1 grams
1 Troy oz = 20 pennyweight (dwt)
1 Pennyweight (dwt) = 1.55 grams
24 Grains = 1 Pennyweight (dwt)
1 Troy lb. = 12 0z.

MEASURES OF LENGTH:
1 inch (1") = 2.54 (cm) centimeters or 25.4 (mm) millimeters
1 foot (1') = 0.305 meters or 30.48 (cm) centimeters = 304.8 (mm) millimeters
1 meter = 39.37 inches
1 (cm) centimeter = 10 millimeters (mm)
10 centimeters (cm) = 1 decimeter (dcm) or 100 millimeters (mm)
100 centimeters (cm) = 1 meter or 10 decimeters (dcm)

The following chart is intended to summarize the types of adhesives available for solderless bonding. Best results are only obtained when the surfaces to be joined are thoroughly clean, and when the manufacturer's directions are carefully followed.

TO BOND	TYPE OF GLUE	APPLICATION	SOLVENT
Porous Materials: Wood, Paper, Fabric, Feathers	Organic: "White Glue" (Elmer's, Sobo, Tacky)*	Clamp. Allow overnight setting.	Water
Plastic, Wood, Leather, Metal, Stone, China, Glass, Shells, Cork	"Household Cement" (Duco, 527, Mascot, Barge, Bonds)*	Rough up surfaces. Apply one coat to each surface. Clamp	Acetone (Nail polish remover)
All Metals, Stone, China, Glass, Shell	Epoxy Cement (Devcon, Duro, Miracle, #330)*	Rough up surfaces. Stir Resin & Hardener on disposable surface. Allow overnight setting.	Mineral Spirits. (Petroleum Solvent)
Metal to Metal, Stone & Glass to Metal. (Not for porous materials)	Alpha Cyanoacrylate (Aron Alpha, Eastman 910, Super Glue, Krazy Glue, Permabond, Zapa Gap)*	Rough up surfaces. Apply to one surface. Bonds instantly. Refrigerate for shelf life.	Dimethyl-Formamide. "Attack"*
Plexiglass, Plastics	Solvent Cement Ethylene Dichloride (Cadco 94, Amco 110)*	Apply around all edges. Clamp together.	None. Plastics are "welded" by softening

* Indicates brand names of adhesives

BIBLIOGRAPHY

Aldred, Cyril
"JEWELS OF THE PHARAOHS"
Ballantine Books - 1978

Arem, Joel
"COLOR ENCYCLOPEDIA OF
GEMSTONES"
Van Nostrand Reinhold - 1977

Ashley, Clifton
"THE BOOK OF KNOTS"
Doubleday & Co. - 1944

Baker, M.L.
"THE ABC'S OF CANVAS
EMBROIDERY"
Old Sturbridge Inc. - 1968

Beck, Horace
"THE CLASSIFICATION & NOMEN-
CLATURE OF BEAD & PENDANTS"
Shumway - 1981

Dubin, Lois S.
"THE HISTORY OF BEADS"
Harry N. Abrams - 1987

Edwards, Joan
"BEAD EMBROIDERY"
Taplinger Publishing Co. - 1969

Erikson, J.M.
"THE UNIVERSAL BEAD"
 Norton - 1979

Fisch, Arlene
"TEXTILE TECHNIQUES IN
METAL"
Van Nostrand Rheinhold -1975

Fisher, Angela
"AFRICA ADORNED"
Harry N. Abrams - 1984

Francis, Peter
"A SHORT DICTIONARY OF BEAD
TERMS & TYPES"
Lapis Route - 1982

Harris, Elizabeth
"A BEAD PRIMER"
The Bead Museum - 1987

Hart, Arnold (Editor)
"JEWELRY: A PICTORIAL ARCHIVE
OF WOODCUTS & ENGRAVINGS"
Dover - 1981

Kliot, Jules & Kaethe (Editors)
"BEADWORK"
Lacis Publications - 1984

LaCroix, Grethe
"CREATING WITH BEADS"
Sterling Publishing Co. - 1969

McCreight, Tim
"METALWORKING FOR JEWELRY"
Van Nostrand Reinhold Co. - 1979

Neumann, Robert
"THE DESIGN & CREATION OF
JEWELRY"
Chilton Book Co. - 1962

O'Connor, Harold
"THE JEWELER'S BENCH
REFERENCE"
Dunconor -1975

Orchard, Wm.C.
"BEADS AND BEADWORK OF THE
AMERICAN INDIANS"
Heye Foundation-Museum of the
American Indian -1929

Pack, Greta
"CHAINS AND BEADS"
Van Nostrand Co. -1952

Poris, Ruth F.
"STEP BY STEP BEAD STRINGING"
Golden Hands Press -1984

Schuman, Walter
"GEMSTONES OF THE WORLD"
Sterling Publishing Co. - 1977

Seyd, Mary
"INTRODUCING BEADS"
Watson-Guptil -1973

Van Der Sleen, W.G.N.
"A HANDBOOK ON BEADS"
Shumway Publishing - 1964

MAGAZINES

AMERICAN CRAFT
A bimonthly craft publication of the
American Craft Council
40 West 53 Street
New York, New York 10019
(212) 956-3535
Lois Moran, Editor

ORNAMENT
A quarterly publication entirely devoted
to ornament.
P.O.Box 2349
San Marcos, Ca. 92069
(800) 888-8950
R. K. Liu, Ph.D., Editor

FOR FURTHER STUDY

THE BEAD MUSEUM
140 South Montezuma
Prescott, Arizona 86301
(602) 445-2431
Gabrielle Liese, Director

CENTER FOR BEAD RESEARCH
4 Essex Street
Lake Placid, N. Y. 12946
(518) 523-1794
Peter Francis, Director

CENTER FOR STUDY OF
BEADWORK
2075 N.W. Glisan (P.O.Box 13719)
Portland. Oregon 97213
(503) 249-1848
Alice Scherer, Director

INDEX